SATAN'S FIRST LIE

Exposing Global Myths About Death, Ghosts, and the Afterlife

STEVE WOHLBERG

The serpent said to the woman, "You will not surely die. For God knows that in the day you eat of it your eyes will be opened, and you will be like God, knowing good and evil." Genesis 3:4, 5

Present Truth Publications
Priest River, Idaho 83856

Photography and cover design by Jaime Galvez

Copyright © Present Truth Publications

Printed in the United States of America
All rights reserved

The author assumes full responsibility for the accuracy of all facts and quotations as cited in this book.

All scripture verses taken from the New King James Version (NKJV), except where indicated as the King James Version (KJV), which is in the public domain.

New King James Version®. Copyright © 1982 by Thomas Nelson. Used by permission. All rights reserved.

You can obtain additional copies of this book by calling toll-free 1-800-765-6955 or by visiting AdventistBookCenter.com.

Library of Congress Cataloging-in-Publication Data

ISBN: 9-798988-756002

First printing: August 2023

Dedicated to all sincere seekers after truth

CONTENTS

Author's Introduction	7
Chapter 1: Immortal Souls	11
Chapter 2: Seduced by a Serpent	15
Chapter 3: Barred From the Tree of Life	21
Chapter 4: Ghosts, Spirits, Devils	28
Chapter 5: Dark Encounter at En Dor	35
Chapter 6: What Happens at Death?	56
Chapter 7: The Resurrection Factor	65
Chapter 8: Absent From the Body	70
Chapter 9: The Thief on the Cross	77
Chapter 10: Moses and Elijah	82
Chapter 11: Souls Under the Altar	86
Chapter 12: The Hot Topic of Hell	89
Chapter 13: Will Hellfire Burn Forever?	102
Chapter 14: Eternal Flames Extinguished	109
Chapter 15: Worms in Unquenchable Fire	116
Chapter 16: The Rich Man and Lazarus	122
Chapter 17: God's Infinite Love Revealed	129

Author's Introduction

"In this world," Ben Franklin famously said, "nothing is certain except death and taxes." He was right. No matter who we are, the color of our skin, or the size of our bank accounts, a solemn day will finally arrive when our lifeless bodies will be lowered into a cemetery, or cremated, or we will die some other way so nothing is left of us.

Death is unavoidable. We can't escape it.

The big question is: What then?

If you ask 100 different people for their opinion about life beyond the grave, you would probably get 100 different answers. Like rabbits, conflicting ideas about death, souls, ghosts, and the afterlife keep multiplying.

Many firmly believe that at death godly saints soar instantly to a blissful Heaven while wicked sinners plunge into the fires of hell.

Others imagine a holding place called purgatory where people not quite good enough for Heaven, but not quite bad enough for hell, will slowly be purged from their impurities. Still others believe that at death the soul simply sheds a physical body—like a snake exiting its skin—to slip peacefully into the spirit world on the Other Side. Is this true? Can the ghosts of our deceased relatives return to talk with us? What about reincarnation? Can a dead person be reborn as another person, a horse, a cow, or even a mouse? Others are convinced that when we die, that's it. We're just dead forever.

In this book we will consult only one Source:

The Holy Bible

Believe it or not, the Bible is actually the world's all-time bestselling Book. It's a single Book, composed of 66 smaller books. Its 66th book, entitled, "The Revelation," solemnly warns about an invisible fallen fiend referred to as "that old serpent," "the Devil and Satan" who "deceives the whole world." Rev. 12:9.

Deceives the whole world?

If Satan really exists, and if this diabolical entity

AUTHOR'S INTRODUCTION

is truly deceiving "the whole world" today—like the Bible plainly states—then it is reasonable to assume that most people now living on this planet are probably wrong about life's deepest mystery: What happens to dead people.

In the following pages, you will learn that this is exactly the case. You will not only discover what the Holy Book teaches about death, souls, ghosts, and the afterlife, but you will also be enabled to discern one of the greatest delusions ever palmed on the human family by a cruel, cunning foe.

You will understand *Satan's first lie.*

More than this, you will learn about one unique Man who has become history's most famous Truth Teller. Nearly two thousand years ago, He was publicly executed on a cruel cross (for speaking the truth), "died . . . was buried, [and] *rose again* the third day according to the Scriptures." 1 Corinthians 15:3, 4 (emphasis added). That resurrected Man has promised that everyone who believes in Him "should not perish but have everlasting life." John 3:16.

He also said:

> You shall know the truth,
> and the truth will shall make you free.
> John 8:32

SATAN'S FIRST LIE

That Man is Jesus Christ. It is this author's earnest prayer that His words of truth will free you from the lies of the evil one, and give you hope and peace.

CHAPTER 1

IMMORTAL SOULS

Every tree has roots. In the same way, in order to correctly understand the truth about death, souls, ghosts, communicating with dead people, hell, the afterlife, and satanic global delusions, we must first dig beneath the surface to explore *the root topic of immortality.*

"Every soul is immortal," many firmly teach today. At first glance, this doctrine seems as unarguable as the pope being Catholic, and as the rabbi being Jewish. "Two days ago, our dearly beloved sister Brenda (a fictitious name) went home to be with the Lord," ministers often tell tearful congregations after someone dies. "Brenda's suffering is over. She's with God now."

Who would dare doubt such a conclusion, especially if Brenda was a kind person who believed in God?

SATAN'S FIRST LIE

Of course Brenda went to Heaven . . . right?

Try to imagine another scene. It's been a month since Brenda's lifeless body was lowered six feet under the ground. But for the flickering of a few eerie candles, the room is pitch dark. Madam Sophia (another fictitious name)—a psychic medium claiming a gifted ability to contact the deceased—reclines comfortably on a black sofa surrounded by a handful of bereaved relatives who aren't churchgoers. The thick smell of incense fills the air. High above a creepy-looking house where this somber group has gathered, the moon shines full.

A lone dog howls in the distance.

"Whom shall I bring up for you?" Madam Sophia softly inquires. "Brenda Webb," replies Ralph Webb nervously. "Brenda died recently, and we have some questions to ask her." Suddenly, a ghost appears in their midst. "Hello, Ralph," says the spirit, "what would you like to know?" A lengthy conversation ensues between a small group of stunned relatives and a glowing entity from the Other Side who looks like, talks like, and acts just like Brenda Webb.

Sound far-fetched? Actually, it isn't, for similar occurrences are increasingly common. Now notice carefully. In spite of the many differences of belief between the Christian pastor who spoke at Brenda Webb's funeral and the psychic medium Madam Sophia who claimed to contact her ghost, they both hold *one fundamental root idea* in common. Both firmly believe that when people die, *they're not completely dead*. Instead, their invisible, inner essence takes flight to soar somewhere beyond what our physical eyes can see.

This is the belief in an immortal soul. Most human beings across planet Earth accept this theory, including most members of the world's largest religions, such as Roman Catholicism, Protestantism and Islam. It is also believed by most Hindus, Buddhists, pagans, Wiccans, Spiritualists, and occultists. While these religions all differ markedly in their understanding of *where* souls go on the day of death, they *all* believe the root concept that every person has an immortal soul that goes somewhere after one's physical body becomes rigid, cold, and lifeless.

Put your hand over your pacemaker (if you have one), and get ready for a shock. This globally popular immortal soul doctrine actually originated with a mesmerizing voice that spoke through a reptile in the Garden of Eden.

Whose voice was it?

You're about to find out.

Chapter 2

Seduced by a Serpent

At the dawn of time, the Sacred Word reveals:

> And the LORD God planted a garden eastward in Eden, and there He put the man whom He had formed. And out of the ground made the LORD God to grow every tree that is pleasant to the sight, and good for food; *the tree of life* also in the midst of the garden, and *the tree of the knowledge of good and evil*. Gen. 2:8, 9 (emphasis added).

As we shall soon see, the issues surrounding these two trees—"the tree of life" and "the tree of the knowledge of good and evil"—affect us to this day. The very first book of the Bible, the book of Genesis, informs us that after placing the very first created human, Adam, in his beautiful garden home, the King of the Universe issued this solemn warning:

> And the LORD God commanded the man, saying, "Of every tree of the garden you may freely eat, but of the tree of the knowledge of good and evil you shall not eat, for in the day that you eat of it you shall surely die." Gen. 2:16, 17.

Notice carefully the last four words spoken to Adam by God Almighty: "*You shall surely die.*" The Lord didn't tell Adam that if he disobeyed God by eating the forbidden fruit "Only your body will die," but rather, "*You shall surely die.*" To Adam, the word "you" meant "you," signifying his entire person. God even added the word "surely" for extra emphasis. His warning was crystal clear. If Adam (or his wife Eve who was created a bit later) disobeyed His clear command not to eat from "the tree of the knowledge of good and evil," that was it. Period.

"YOU SHALL SURELY DIE," said their Maker.

God's first warning couldn't have been plainer.

The word "die" literally meant that they

would be dead, not alive somewhere else. In North Idaho where my family lives, we often see dead deer on the side of the road. If a deer gets hit hard enough by a passing car, it's over.

That deer is dead.

Yes, *really dead*.

In Genesis chapter 3, the drama begins. Wandering from Adam's watchful side, Eve found herself gazing at the forbidden tree. Suddenly she saw a beautiful, winged serpent slithering among its fruit-laden branches. As she watched it in wonder, amazingly, the serpent spoke. What Eve didn't realize was that this strange creature was a mouthpiece for an invisible fallen angel named Lucifer who had recently been evicted from Heaven (see Isaiah 14:12–14). Unfortunately for Eve (and us), she decided to dialog with this fascinating creature. And what did the serpent say? The Bible reports:

> Then *the serpent said to the woman*, "You will *not surely die*. For God knows that in the day you eat of it [the forbidden fruit] your eyes will be opened, and you will be like God, knowing good and evil." Gen. 3:4, 5 (emphasis added).

Did you catch that? It was "the serpent" that first snickered, "You will not surely die," in direct contrast to God's word. This was *Satan's first lie* ever spoken to a human. *His second lie* was that humans can become little gods. Again, the Lord stated, "You will *surely* die." "No, *you won't*," insisted the Devil. "Instead, you will live on, and on, and on, because you will be like God Himself. Then you won't need to be dependent on God but only on your own self to live forever."

This was the gist of his distorted message.

Tragically, Eve believed the snake, violated God's clear command, took the forbidden fruit, and ate it. Then she offered the fruit to Adam, and he ate, too (see Gen. 3:6). The consequences of their actions have been horrific and have resulted in untold pain, heartache, sorrow, and death for all humanity. Ultimately, those two seemingly tiny acts of disobedience to God's voice led to the death of His own Son on a cruel cross to remedy this terrible problem.

Yes, sin is that serious.

One lesson from this account is that we should always trust *what God says* and reject Satan's lies.

After Adam and Eve sinned, God reiterated

His "You will surely die" message to the guilty pair.

Then to Adam He said . . . "In the sweat of your face you shall eat bread till you return to the ground, for out of it you were taken; *for dust you are, and to dust you shall return.*" Gen. 3:17, 19 (emphasis added).

Notice that God didn't tell Adam that merely his physical body would revert to dust, but that his descent back into the earth applied to his entire being. "For dust *you* are," the Lord clarified, "and to dust *you* shall return." That three-letter word, "you" takes in Adam's entire existence.

To better grasp the meaning of this ancient Bible verse, we must back up to Genesis 2:7 where the Bible first carefully describes the creation of Adam. Look closely:

> And the LORD God formed man of the dust of the ground, and breathed into his nostrils the breath of life; and *man became a living soul.* Gen. 2:7, KJV (emphasis added).

Here the Sacred Record states that Adam was initially formed from "the dust of the ground." First, he was lifeless. Then God "breathed into his nostrils the breath of life." This "breath of life" wasn't a mystic, eerie, out-of-body intelligence, but rather a spark of "life" that God placed into all creation, including animals (see Gen. 7:21, 22 and Psalm 104:29, 30). When "the breath of life" entered Adam's lifeless form, "the man became a living soul."

Notice carefully that God didn't insert a separate soul component into Adam. Instead, Adam "*became* a living soul." He was now alive. *He was a living soul.* At the moment of death (which is the inevitable result of sin) everything reverses. Then "the breath of life" simply returns to God who gave it, and the physical body returns to the ground from which it came (see also Psalm 104:29, 30; Ecclesiastes 12:7).

The big question is: When Adam, Eve, other humans, or even a deer dies, and then their physical bodies return to the dust, does their "breath of life," or "spirit," or "soul" consciously continue into some sort of afterlife? In other words, do fallen, sinful humans have, somewhere deep within their physical bodies, an immortal component, or eternal soul, that consciously survives and continues after death?

SATAN'S FIRST LIE

"Of course! It's a no-brainer," says nearly every religion on Earth.

But is this globally popular idea *really true?*

Remember, the Devil "deceives t*he whole world.*" Rev. 12:9 (emphasis added).

Could this teaching be a repetition of *Satan's first lie?*

Let's find out.

Chapter 3

Barred From the Tree of Life

Shortly after God notified Adam and Eve that because of their sin they would "surely die" and return to the dust, a highly significant scene unfolded:

> Then the LORD God said, "Behold, the man has become like one of Us, to know good and evil. And now, *lest he put out his hand and take also of the tree of life, and eat, and live forever*"—therefore the LORD God sent him out of the Garden of Eden to till the ground from which he was taken. So He drove out the man; and He placed cherubim at the east of the Garden of Eden, and a flaming sword which turned every way, *to guard the way to the tree of life*. Gen. 3:22–24 (emphasis added).

SATAN'S FIRST LIE

From this passage, we learn four facts:

1. Because Adam and Eve sinned against God, they had become fallen sinners capable of knowing both "good and evil."

2. If they were to eat fruit from the tree of life in their sinful state, they would "live forever."

3. This was NOT God's will—for if fallen sinful humans naturally lived forever, then sin itself would exist forever, too. To the Maker of planet Earth and His eternal Son (referred to as "Us" in verse 22), this thought was intolerable.

4. To prevent such a catastrophe, "the LORD God" banished Adam and Eve from their garden home in Eden and then stationed two mighty angels (cherubim) with flaming swords "to guard the way to the tree of life." Gen. 3:24.

The inescapable conclusion from simply reading Genesis 3:22–24 is that Adam and Eve were prevented by two sword-flashing angelic warriors from eating fruit from the tree of life. Therefore, neither they nor any of their descendants (us) *naturally "live forever."* Due to the entrance of sin, we are now "mortal," which means subject to death, not naturally immortal.

When Adam finally died, the Bible reports:

So all the days that Adam *lived* were nine hundred and thirty years; and he *died.* Gen. 5:5 (emphasis added).

This inspired Bible verse is super-simple, if we are humble enough to believe it. For 930 years after his terrible sin, "Adam lived" to regret his awful mistake. Then "he died," just like God said he would. The same thing happens to each of us. Today, we are alive; but someday, we too will die.

In the days of the Old West, posted notices sometimes read, "Wanted: Dead or Alive." Obviously, being dead or alive are two very different states. Wanted outlaws and criminals could be captured in one state (alive) or in the other state (dead), but not both. It was the same with Adam, and it is the same with each of us.

We're either dead, or alive.

We can't be both.

SATAN'S FIRST LIE

When Adam "died," biblically speaking, his "soul" ceased to exist too, simply because, when God first breathed "the breath of life" into him, he "*became* a living soul." Gen. 2:7, KJV. In other words, souls are real people, not bodiless spirit entities. Here's more proof:

When Joshua conquered Eglon, "*all the souls* that were therein he utterly destroyed that day." Joshua 10:35, KJV (emphasis added). This doesn't mean Joshua slew some mystical inner parts of his enemies, but simply that he killed real people in Eglon. He did the same in Hebron. He "smote it with the edge of the sword, and the king thereof, and all the cities thereof, and *all the souls* that were therein." Verse 37, KJV (emphasis added). And in Debir: "they smote them with the edge of the sword, and *utterly destroyed all the souls* that were therein." Verse 39, KJV (emphasis added).

On the Day of Atonement, which was to be sacredly observed by the Israelites in the Promised Land, God warned that "*whatsoever soul* it be that doeth any work in that same day, *the same soul will I destroy from among his people*." Lev. 23:30, KJV (emphasis added). Thus souls are destructible, not indestructible.

When Paul sailed to Rome, there were "in

the ship two hundred threescore [260] and sixteen *souls*." Acts 27:37, KJV (emphasis added). This doesn't mean 276 spooky apparitions floated above waves, but simply, as the New King James Version states, that there were "two hundred and seventy-six persons on the ship." Acts 27:37 (emphasis added).

Because Adam and Eve sinned against God, fallen human beings (living souls) now exist in a "mortal" state:

> Shall *mortal man* be more just than God? Job 4:17, KJV (emphasis added).

The Bible also plainly teaches that *only God* is immortal. The New Testament describes Him as:

> The King of kings and Lord of lords, *who alone has immortality,* dwelling in unapproachable light, whom no man has seen or can see, to whom be honor andeverlasting power. Amen. 1 Tim. 6:15, 16 (emphasis added).

As fallen sinners, we must "*seek* for glory, honor, and *immortality*." Romans 2:7 (emphasis added). Think about it. If we must "seek"

SATAN'S FIRST LIE

for immortality, then it's obvious that we don't have immortality right now. But when Jesus Christ returns to raise His people from the dead, then will "this mortal put on immortality." 1 Corinthians 15:53.

Thus the Bible's message is NOT that when people die their invisible, immortal souls instantly exit their bodies to blast off into outer space. Not at all. Instead, as with Adam, people live, then they die. First they're alive, then they're dead. Finally, in the future, comes "a resurrection of the dead, both of the just and unjust." Acts 24:15.

"A lie can travel half-way around the world," stated the witty Mark Twain, "before truth puts its boots on." According to God's Word, the "immortal soul" doctrine is one of those lies. Yes, it's popular; yes, millions believe it; and yes, it's taught by Big Religion, but the fact is that this teaching was first introduced by the crafty serpent in Eden. Even worse, it was *Satan's first lie*. Tragically, Eve believed that lie, and so do most people today, including psychic mediums like Madam Sophia, and even most pastors and priests.

Here's the scary part. If people truly believe that their deceased loved ones aren't really dead, but are alive somewhere in the spirit world, this makes them particularly vulnerable to being seduced by spooky spirits claiming to be the ghosts of dead people.

Who are those spirits?

What does God's Book really say?

CHAPTER 4

GHOSTS, SPIRITS, DEVILS

A few years ago I sat on a United Airlines flight traveling from Chicago to Los Angeles. Suddenly, a friendly-looking commercial popped onto a large screen in the main cabin. An attractive blonde woman stood cooking in the kitchen. These words appeared: "6:30 AM, prepare breakfast for the family." The scene changed, and this sentence appeared: "7:30 AM, send the kids off to school." After another scene change, these words popped up: "9:30 AM, clean the house." Finally, the punchline appeared: "11:00 AM, talk to the dead." Viewers were then invited to watch the TV series "Medium, 9:00–10:00 PM CT on NBC."

Everything appeared so homey and innocent.

The notion of talking to dead people isn't just Hollywood fiction either. In the 1960s,

GHOSTS, SPIRITS, DEVILS

a woman named Jane Roberts encountered a mysterious, invisible entity while she and her husband dabbled with a Ouija board in their New York apartment. The spirit—who said his name was "Seth"—later took full possession of Jane's body and even dictated volumes of information through her fingers that eventually became known as "The Seth Material." These weren't fictitious encounters, or merely the product of Jane Robert's wild imagination. No indeed. In fact, many of these encounters were witnessed firsthand by hundreds of astonished researchers.*

When under Seth's influence, Jane's face changed dramatically. A man's voice spoke through her lips. The final verdict of astonished observers was that the Seth entity—who claimed to be the ghost of a dead person—was definitely *not Jane Roberts*.

A real spirit was speaking from the Other Side.

Of course, the notion of talking to dead people has been around for centuries, but it has usually been relegated to séances in dimly lit rooms, or to isolated instances. But in the last 25 years or so, fueled by countless

---

* See https://en.wikipedia.org/wiki/Jane_Roberts.

SATAN'S FIRST LIE

talking-to-the-dead Hollywood movies, TV series, documentaries, and *New York Times* bestselling books written by real-life psychic mediums, the idea has gone mainstream.

The creepy trend continues to this day.

To be fair, losing a loved one or close friend is incredibly painful, and it's natural to wish they were still here. It's also perfectly normal to long to hear their voice and feel their touch. But is trying to contact them a safe endeavor? Is this the best way to receive comfort?

Make no mistake about it: *Real spirits* do inhabit our atmosphere, and they often *claim* to be the spirits of dead people. But are they really? Our family used to have a housekeeper named Mary who candidly told us that after her husband died his spirit visited her. "I saw him myself," Mary reported. "His spirit walked right through the screen door into my bedroom and talked to me!" Was it really her dead husband? How can we know? Just because a spirit looks, talks, and acts like a dead person, is this irrefutable proof that it really is that person?

Everyone knows that humans often lie.

Is it possible that spirits might lie, too?

Paul wrote, "We walk by faith, not by sight." 2 Cor. 5:7. This means that whatever our thoughts, feelings, eyes, or other senses tell us, we should trust God and His Word first and foremost. This is the biblical position. It is also where Adam and Eve (humanity's first parents) failed. "He who trusts in his own heart is a fool" (Proverbs 28:26), wrote King Solomon, acknowledged to be the wisest men who ever lived. So what about talking to dead people? Get ready for another shock:

The Bible categorically forbids all communication with the spirits of dead people.

Here's the proof. In Deuteronomy 18:9–11, God listed numerous occult practices that His ancient people were to avoid like the Black Plague. "When you come into the land," God told the Israelites, "you shall not learn to follow the abominations of those nations." "What abominations?" you might ask. Notice carefully: "There shall not be found among you anyone . . . who conjures spells or a medium, or a *spiritist*, or *one who calls up the dead*. For all who do these things are an abomination to the LORD." Verses 10, 11 (emphasis added). Again God warned, "Give no regard to *mediums* and *familiar spirits*; do not seek after them, to be defiled by them: I am the LORD your God." Lev. 19:31 (emphasis added).

These Bible verses are crystal clear. God forbids any involvement with "mediums," "spiritists," or those *trying to contact the dead.* Psychic mediums, Hollywood TV series, the Seth Material, *New York Times* bestselling authors, and countless others may promote this practice, but God emphatically warns,

"Don't do it!"

Why not? Is He trying to prevent us from finding comfort, or receiving real guidance from deceased loved ones? No. His reason is simple. Mysterious nonphysical entities may look like, talk like, and act like the dead, but according to a careful study of the Book of books—*they aren't the dead.*

Who are they, then?

The Book of Revelation lifts the veil by declaring: "They are *the spirits of devils*, working miracles, which go forth unto the kings of the Earth and of the whole world, to gather them to the battle of that great Day of God Almighty." Rev. 16:14, KJV (emphasis added). In plain language, the last book of the Bible solemnly warns us not to be misled by the supernatural activities of real "spirits of devils" (fallen angels evicted with Lucifer from

GHOSTS, SPIRITS, DEVILS

Heaven) that will perform signs, wonders, and miracles worldwide right before the Day of the Lord.

Some of these miracles are happening right now.

God doesn't use such forceful language because He hates us. Not at all. In fact, He even cares about psychic mediums and spiritists. Instead, the reason He speaks so strongly is because He loves us and longs to protect us from the malicious power of "the Devil and his angels" (Matthew 25:41) who can easily personate dead people.

Many ancient medieval churches still standing in England have one special door built into their north side called "The Devil's Door." Reasons for this ancient tradition vary, but one thing's for sure. If people today believe in the immortal soul doctrine, such a belief can easily become "The Devil's Door" into deadly encounters with Lucifer's legions whose ultimate goal is to kill and to destroy us (see John 10:10).

God's Word sounds a warning because He doesn't want us to have "fellowship with devils." 1 Cor. 10:20, KJV. Instead, He offers us a safer path. "I am come that they might have life," Jesus said, "and that they might have it more abundantly. I am the good shepherd: the good shepherd gives His life for the sheep." John 10:10, 11.

The Truth Teller loves us and even sacrificed His life on a cruel cross to win our hearts back to loyalty to God. But if we reject His solemn warnings against dialoging with the deceased, which can bring us into contact with demons, to put it bluntly, we don't have a ghost of a chance.

Chapter 5

Dark Encounter at En Dor

We have seen that the Bible strongly forbids all attempts to communicate with the dead (Lev. 19:31; Deut. 18:11). There are two primary reasons for these sober warnings: 1) Demons can easily personate the deceased, thereby tricking the living into communicating with them; and 2) It is impossible for the dead to talk with the living anyway. This latter point will become clearer soon.

Yet there is one chapter in the Bible that has confused many readers, 1 Samuel 28, which—on the surface—seems to teach that the ghost of the dead prophet Samuel did return to communicate with King Saul. Let's take a close look. First we'll read the entire section, verses 3-25. Then we will examine the details.

SATAN'S FIRST LIE

3 Now Samuel had died, and all Israel had lamented for him and buried him in Ramah, in his own city. And Saul had put the mediums and the spiritists out of the land.

4 Then the Philistines gathered together, and came and encamped at Shunem. So Saul gathered all Israeltogether, and they encamped at Gilboa.

5 When Saul saw the army of the Philistines, he was afraid, and his heart trembled greatly.

6 And when Saul inquired of the LORD, the LORD did not answer him, either by dreams or by Urim or by the prophets.

7 Then Saul said to his servants, "Find me a woman who is a medium, that I may go to her and inquire of her." And his servants said to him, "In fact, there is a woman who is a medium at En Dor."

8 So Saul disguised himself and put on other clothes, and he went, and two men with him; and they came to the woman

by night. And he said, "Please conduct a séance for me, and bring up for me the one I shall name to you."

9 Then the woman said to him, "Look, you know what Saul has done, how he has cut off the mediums and the spiritists from the land. Why then do you lay a snare for my life, to cause me to die?"

10 And Saul swore to her by the LORD, saying, "As the LORD lives, no punishment shall come upon you for this thing."

11 Then the woman said, "Whom shall I bring up for you?" And he said, "Bring up Samuel for me."

12 When the woman saw Samuel, she cried out with a loud voice. And the woman spoke to Saul, saying, "Why have you deceived me? For you are Saul!"

13 And the king said to her, "Do not be afraid. What did you see?" And the woman said to Saul, "I saw a spirit ascending out of the earth."

SATAN'S FIRST LIE

14 So he said to her, "What is his form?" And she said, "An old man is coming up, and he is covered with a mantle." And Saul perceived that it was Samuel, and he stooped with his face to the ground and bowed down.

15 Now Samuel said to Saul, "Why have you disturbed me by bringing me up?" And Saul answered, "I am deeply distressed; for the Philistines make war against me, and God has departed from me and does not answer me anymore, neither by prophets nor by dreams. Therefore I have called you, that you may reveal to me what I should do."

16 Then Samuel said: "So why do you ask me, seeing the LORD has departed from you and has become your enemy?

17 And the LORD has done for Himself as He spoke by me. For the LORD has torn the kingdom out of your hand and given it to your neighbor, David.

18 Because you did not obey the voice of the LORD nor execute His fierce wrath

upon Amalek, therefore the LORD has done this thing to you this day.

19 Moreover the LORD will also deliver Israel with you into the hand of the Philistines. And tomorrow you and your sons will be with me. The LORD will also deliver the army of Israel into the hand of the Philistines."

20 Immediately Saul fell full length on the ground, and was dreadfully afraid because of the words of Samuel. And there was no strength in him, for he had eaten no food all day or all night.

21 And the woman came to Saul and saw that he was severely troubled, and said to him, "Look, your maidservant has obeyed your voice, and I have put my life in my hands and heeded the words which you spoke to me.

22 "Now therefore, please, heed also the voice of your maidservant, and let me set a piece of bread before you; and eat, that you may have strength when you go on your way."

23 But he refused and said, "I will not eat." So his servants, together with the woman, urged him; and he heeded their voice. Then he arose from the ground and sat on the bed.

24 Now the woman had a fatted calf in the house, and she hastened to kill it. And she took flour and kneaded it, and baked unleavened bread from it.

25 So she brought it before Saul and his servants, and they ate. Then they rose and went away that night.

Let's analyze this chapter section, point by point. After the elderly prophet Samuel "had died," a vast Philistine army gathered together against King Saul and the Israelites. When Saul realized how ferocious the Philistine forces were, "his heart trembled greatly." Close to the end of his kingly career, this unfortunate leader had strayed far from God. When Samuel was still alive, King Saul had stubbornly ignored his instructions (see 1 Samuel 15). The present situation was ominous. Hoping against hope for heavenly help in this emergency, "Saul inquired of the LORD, [but] the Lord did not answer him, either by dreams or by Urim or by the prophets." Don't miss this point. Whatever happened next, it wasn't God or *one of His prophets* who spoke to Saul.

For many years King Saul had persistently rejected God's tender appeals, so the Lord now decided that He would not respond like a busboy to Saul's desperate pleas. In the book of Proverbs, God made His position plain:

> Because I have called and you refused,
> I have stretched out My hand and
>   no one regarded,
> Because you disdained all My counsel,
> And would have none of My rebuke,
> I also will laugh at your calamity;
> I will mock when your terror comes,
> When your terror comes like a storm,
> And your destruction comes like a
>   whirlwind,
> When distress and anguish come
>   upon you.
> Then they will call on Me, but I will
>   not answer;
> They will seek Me diligently, but they
>   will not find Me. Proverbs 1:24–28.

SATAN'S FIRST LIE

Unfortunately, this was Saul's miserable plight. Heaven was silent. In this crisis hour, "Saul said to his servants, 'Find me a woman who is a medium, that I may go to her and inquire of her.' And his servants said to him, 'In fact, there is a woman who is a medium at En Dor.' " Matthew Henry, the author of one of the most respected Bible commentaries in church history, commented,

> Saul seeks for a witch, v. 7. When God *answered him not*, if he had humbled himself by repentance and persevered in seeking God, who knows but that at length He might have been entreated for him? but, since he can discern no comfort either from Heaven or Earth (Isa. 8:21, 22), he resolves to knock at the gates of hell, and to see if any there will befriend him and give him advice: Seek me a woman that has a familiar spirit, v. 7.*

King Saul knew what Moses wrote in Deuteronomy 18, and by judicial authority he had even previously "put the mediums and the

---

* See https://www.christianity.com/bible/commentary/matthew-henry-complete/1-samuel/28. All emphases in the original.

Dark Encounter at En Dor

spiritists out of the land." But a few remained in hiding, and his servants remembered that there was a woman who practiced magic arts inside a cave at En Dor. So, taking two men with him, Saul disguised himself and "came to the woman by night."

What a pitiful scene! Israel's king, a man chosen to represent God on Earth, disguises himself and, under cover of darkness, creeps like a lizard into a cave. Matthew Henry continues bluntly,

> Hearing of one [a witch or oracle] he [King Saul] hastens to her, but goes by night, and in disguise, only with two servants, and probably on foot, v. 8. See how those that are led captive by Satan are forced, 1. To disparage themselves. Never did Saul look so mean as when he went sneaking to a sorry witch to know his fortune. 2. To dissemble. Evil works are works of darkness, and they hate the light, neither care for coming to it. Saul went to the witch, not in his robes, but in the habit of a common soldier, not only lest the witch herself, if she had known him, should decline to serve him, either fearing he came to trepan [archaism

for entrap, lure] her or resolving to be avenged on him for his edict against those of her profession, but lest his own people should know it and abhor him for it. Such is the power of natural conscience that eventhose who do evil blush and are ashamed to do it.

Upon finding the woman, Saul pleaded, "Please conduct a séance for me, and bring up for me the one I shall name to you." Take note of this. Whoever or whatever is about to appear, it materialized at the command of a witch during a séance. This fact alone excludes the possibility that the ghostly entity who entered that cave was the real prophet Samuel.

Upon perceiving his request, the woman trembled. Was this a trap? She reminded this stranger (whom she as yet didn't recognize) of King Saul's own edict against wizards and mediums, which surely must have stabbed the king's conscience. Here was a witch reminding him of his own law! The woman's comment, "Look, you know what Saul has done, how he has cut off the mediums and the spiritists of the land," teaches an important lesson. Matthew Henry writes:

Observe how sensible she is of danger from the edict of Saul, and what care she is in to guard against it; but not at all apprehensive of the obligations of God's law and the terrors of His wrath. She considered what Saul had done, not what God had done, against such practices, and feared a snare laid for her life more than a snare laid for her soul.

Saul assured the woman that no harm would befall her. So, she began preparing her incantations, "Then the woman said, 'Whom shall I bring up for you?' And he said, 'Bring up Samuel for me.' " Again, keep in mind that whoever or whatever is about to appear in the eerie illumination of flickering candles, it responded to the summons of a spiritualistic medium in a dark mountain cave during a séance.

We don't know what spells or charms the witch used, but we do know that suddenly a ghostly apparition entered that clammy cave, and also that at this exact moment the medium received the shock of her life. "And the woman spoke to Saul, saying, "Why have you deceived me? For you are Saul!" How did she suddenly know this? There is no hint in the sacred text that she had visually penetrated the king's disguise. Matthew Henry insightfully writes:

> The witch, upon sight of the apparition, was aware that her client was Saul, her familiar spirit, it is likely, informing her of it (v. 12).

Saul sought to calm her fears. "The king said to her, 'Do not be afraid. What did you see?'" It's important to note that throughout this eerie encounter Saul himself never saw the spirit conjured by the medium. Only the woman did. The same thing often occurs when modern mediums give spiritual "readings" to their "clients," or visit haunted houses seeking ghosts. The subtitle for the old *CBS Ghost Whisperer* series declared that mediums "see what others can't." In her book *Visits from the Afterlife*, psychic medium Sylvia Browne reported that often, even while the TV cameras were rolling, she alone suddenly perceived the presence of a ghost, while nobody else did. The crew may have felt a creepy chill, yet they didn't physically witness anything beyond equipment, cameras, and furniture.

Dark Encounter at En Dor

The same thing happened inside that dark cave before King Saul and his men.

"The woman said to Saul, 'I saw a spirit ascending out of the earth.'" Then Saul inquired, "What is his form?" This again proves that Saul never saw the apparition; only the medium did. "And she said, 'An old man is coming up, and he is covered with a mantle.'" Now notice carefully the next sentence, "And Saul perceived that it was Samuel, and he stooped with his face to the ground and bowed down" (emphasis added). Was it really Samuel? Saul thought so, but did that make it so? Keep in mind that the pitiable king's spiritual perceptions were quite dull at the time. Beyond this, think logically with me: Even if it were possible (more on this later) for the dead to return to talk to the living, would the spirit of the real prophet Samuel appear in a clammy cave at the beckoning of a witch? Hardly! Here's Matthew Henry's sober conclusion:

> God permitted the devil, to answer the design, to put on Samuel's shape, that those who would not *receive the love of the truth* might be *given up to strong delusions* and believe a lie. . . . That the devil, by

the divine permission, should be able to personate Samuel is not strange, since he can *transform himself into an angel of light!* nor is it strange that he should be permitted to do it upon this occasion, that Saul might be driven to despair, by enquiring of the devil, since he would not, in a right manner, enquire of the Lord, by which he might have had comfort.

Pastor Henry's sober assessment fits the scriptural evidence. It was a demon in disguise that appeared to a witch in that cave. The entity then asked Saul, "Why have you disturbed me by bringing me up?" Saul then described the Philistine threat, his dire situation, and the Lord's refusal to answer him by dreams or prophets. "Therefore I have called you," Saul told the ghost, "that you may reveal to me what I should do." A shameful dialog then occurs between an evil spirit and the King of Israel. Matthew Henry notes,

We have here the conference between Saul and Satan. Saul came in disguise (v. 8), but Satan soon discovered him, v. 12. Satan comes in disguise, in the disguise of Samuel's mantle, and Saul cannot discover him. Such is the disadvantage we labour under, in wrestling with *the rulers of the darkness of this world*, that they know us, while we are ignorant of their wiles and devices.

The apparition of Samuel coldly replied (verses 16–18):

"So why do you ask me, seeing the LORD has departed from you and has become your enemy? And the LORD has done for Himself as He spoke by me. For the LORD has torn the kingdom out of your hand and given it to your neighbor, David.

"Because you did not obey the voice of the LORD nor execute His fierce wrath upon Amalek, therefore the LORD has done this thing to you this day."

This passage contains important lessons. The ghostly entity referenced specific past events and even quoted exact statements previously made by the prophet Samuel (when he was alive) about Saul's disobedience and about God's choice of someone else (a modest, obscure shepherd boy named David) to replace Saul as Israel's king. This shows that demons have an intelligent awareness of specific events in people's past and that they will utilize this knowledge as part of their trickery. Modern mediums: Take heed! Just because an invisible being knows intimate details about a deceased person, this isn't proof it is really that person. It only proves that the particular spirit is smart—but not necessarily honest.

Impersonating Samuel, the lying spirit claimed, "The LORD . . . spoke by me," which implied that God was again speaking to Saul through His deceased prophet. But this is impossible, for the Bible specifically states that God was no longer speaking to Saul by His prophets (see 1 Samuel 28:6). Therefore this ghost was not Samuel the prophet. Here is Matthew Henry's penetrating analysis:

> Yet, to make him believe that he was Samuel, the apparition affirmed that it was God who spoke by him. The devil knows how to speak with an air of religion, and can teach false apostles to transform themselves into the apostles of Christ and imitate their language. Those who use spells and charms, and plead, in

defense of them, that they find nothing in them but what is good, may remember what good words the devil here spoke, and yet with what a malicious design.

"Moreover," the demon declared, "the LORD will also deliver Israel with you into the hand of the Philistines. And tomorrow you and your sons will be with me. The LORD will also deliver the army of Israel into the hand of the Philistines." Verse 19. This is precisely what happened (see 1 Sam. 31). Thus demons can—in a limited sense—sometimes foretell the future. Those who trust fortune tellers ought to be aware of this. Just because a person, or spirit, accurately predicts a few pending events, this is no proof of divine inspiration. Even with sin-corrupted minds, Lucifer and his devil comrades aren't stupid. They've existed for centuries, are keen observers, and can even make certain events occur to fulfill their "predictions." In Saul's case, Satan knew God had departed from the wandering king, had withdrawn His protection, and that now he himself had Saul under his power.

"Immediately Saul fell full length on the ground, and was dreadfully afraid because of the words of Samuel. And there was no strength in him, for he had eaten no food all day or all night." Verse 20. Earlier in this dark dialog Saul had asked the entity he *perceived* to be Samuel what he should do; but now he received no helpful guidance—only a bleak prediction of approaching doom for himself and his sons. This response snuffed out Saul's last flicker of hope. As the insightful commentator Henry observes,

> Satan had helped him to palliate and excuse that sin when Samuel was dealing with him to bring him to repentance, but now he aggravates it, to make him despair of God's mercy. See what those get that hearken to Satan's temptations. He himself will be their accuser, and insult over them [triumph over with insolence and contempt].

The doomed king staggered to his feet, gulped down some food, "Then," with his servants, "rose and went away that night." Verse 25. The next day his three sons lay dead on the battlefield, and he was mortally wounded. As the Philistines advanced for the kill, Saul realized all hope was lost, so he committed suicide to avoid being captured and tortured. "So Saul, his three sons, his armorbearer, and all his men died together that same day." 1 Sam. 31:6.

The Bible summary sadly reads: "So Saul died for his unfaithfulness which he had committed against the LORD, because he did not keep the word of the LORD, and also because he consulted a medium for guidance." 1 Chronicles 10:13 (emphasis added).

Such was the miserable, bitter end of a man who rejected God's counsel and sought assistance from a ghost in a cave. Echoing down the corridors of time, this message from the ancient prophet Isaiah speaks to our generation:

> When they say to you, "Seek those who are mediums and wizards, who whisper and mutter," should not a people seek their God? Should they seek the dead on behalf of the living? To the law and to the testimony! If they do not speak according to this Word, *it is because there is no light in them.* Isa. 8:19, 20 (emphasis added).

Isaiah said we must choose whom we will "seek." The options are plain. We can seek the living God or "the dead." We can trust familiar spirits who "whisper and mutter," or the "Word" of our loving Creator. Isaiah also clarified that every teaching should be closely compared with "the law" (the writings of Moses) and "the testimony" (of God's prophets) to test its validity. When any professed teacher disagrees with God's Book, we can be sure "there is no light in them." Isa. 8:20.

Don't be fooled.

Beware of demons in disguise.

Bible truth alone is our safeguard against invisible personalities who may talk kindly, but whose ultimate agenda is either to push human beings toward their death (as with King Saul), or to turn them into lunatics who inhabit cemeteries (see Mark chapter 5). On the other hand, Satan seems content to allow most mediums to retain their sanity for a while (like the witch in the cave) and even to prosper financially. But it's all a trap. He's just biding his time while becoming more sure of his victims.

I will close this chapter with an eye-opening quotation. If you log onto the Internet and find the Merriam-Webster.com online dictionary, try typing in the words, "familiar spirit" into the "Search Dictionary" field. I did it recently. Two definitions are listed. The second one reads: "the spirit of a dead person invoked by a medium to advise or prophesy."

Now "the spirit of a dead person" is precisely what modern psychic mediums claim to encounter in their séances and seminars. But it is the first dictionary definition that should rattle their souls. When I first read it, I could scarcely believe my eyes. Take a look. The first definition of a "familiar spirit" is "a spirit or demon that serves or prompts an individual."*

This is my point exactly.

---

* See https://www.merriam-webster.com/dictionary/familiar%20spirit.

CHAPTER 6

WHAT HAPPENS AT DEATH?

Our journey continues.

Our next question is: What does the Bible really say happens at the moment of death? Surprisingly, the answer is simple, reasonable, understandable, and quite clear; that is, if we are willing to accept what God says. Notice carefully:

> For the living know that they will die; *but the dead know nothing.* . . . Also their love, their hatred, and their envy have now perished; nevermore will they have a share in anything done under the sun. . . . Whatever your hand finds to do, do it with your might; *for there is no work or device or knowledge or wisdom in the grave where you are going.* Eccl. 9:5, 6, 10 (emphasis added).

WHAT HAPPENS AT DEATH?

For in death there is no remembrance of You; in the grave who will give You thanks? Ps. 6:5.

The dead do not praise the LORD, *nor any who go down into silence.* Ps. 115:17 (emphasis added).

[When a person dies] his breath goeth forth, he returneth to his earth; in that very day his thoughts perish. Ps. 146:4 (KJV, emphasis added).

These easy-to-grasp verses plainly teach that after death a dead person knows nothing, has no thoughts, doesn't remember God, and lies silent in the grave.

This is the Word of the Lord, not man's opinion.

The Bible also compares death to going to sleep. The psalmist wrote about "the sleep of death." Ps. 13:3. All throughout the Old Testament, when kings died and were buried, they "slept with their fathers." 1 Kings 2:10. This teaching is often repeated in the New Testament. When His friend Lazarus died, our Savior said, "Our friend Lazarus sleeps. . . . However, Jesus spoke of his death." John

11:11, 13. After Stephen was martyred, "he fell asleep." Acts 7:60. Dead Christians "sleep in Jesus." 1 Thessalonians 4:14. The Old Testament prophet Daniel also wrote that at the end of the world, "many who sleep in the dust of the earth shall awake, some to everlasting life, and some to shame and everlasting contempt." Daniel 12:2. Thus, according to both the Old and New Testaments, those who have died in the past are now *silently sleeping in the dust of the earth.*

Thankfully, that's not the end of the story.
Someday they will wake up. But when?
When Jesus Christ returns!

The apostle Paul—who penned most of the New Testament—clarified this exact point in his first letter to a Christian church located in the Greek city of Thessalonica. In those early days of Christian history, most new converts thought that Jesus Christ would return during their lifetime. But He tarried. As the years went by, one by one, many of these early believers sank to their graves, which elicited the burning question among those who remained, what would happen to their deceased friends?

Were they gone forever?
Much confusion persisted.

What Happens at Death?

So Paul addressed this issue in 1 Thessalonians 4:13–18. Follow closely. In verse 13, he wrote, "I do not want you to be ignorant, brethren, concerning those who have fallen asleep, lest you sorrow as others who have no hope." So far, Paul's main points are: 1) We shouldn't be "ignorant" of this vital topic; 2) Those who had died had merely "fallen asleep"; 3) Those still living shouldn't sorrow like worldly people "who have no hope."

In verse 14, Paul continued: "For if we believe that Jesus died and rose again, even so God will bring with Him those who sleep in Jesus." This verse has confused some people today into thinking that the spirits of believers instantly soar to Heaven at death only to return "with" Jesus (when He returns) to reenter their resurrected bodies. But such an interpretation is highly strained. A closer look at the text will make Paul's meaning crystal clear.

First, he points to Jesus Christ's own death and resurrection: "Jesus died and rose again" because God brought Christ up from the grave. "Even so," Paul continues, "God will bring" u*p from their graves* those presently "sleeping in Jesus" *when Christ returns.*

An honest reading of the next few verses

leaves no doubt that this is precisely what Paul meant. In verse 15, Paul declared: "For this we say to you by the word of the Lord, that we who are alive and remain until the coming of the Lord will by no means precede those who are asleep." In other words, when Jesus returns to gather His people, those who had died first won't ascend first, nor will those who are alive at that glorious moment enter Heaven before the sleeping dead. Instead, both groups will ascend to Heaven together *at the same time.*

Paul continued:

For the Lord Himself shall descend from Heaven with a shout, with the voice of the Archangel, and with the trump of God: and the dead in Christ shall rise first: then we which are alive and remain shall be caught up together with them in the clouds, to meet the Lord in the air: and *so shall we ever be with the Lord.* 1 Thess. 4:16, 17, KJV (emphasis added).

Here Paul clarified that "the dead in Christ" aren't high above us, peering down. Instead, they are below our feet, but they "shall rise" at the resurrection of the dead. At the same time, living believers "shall be caught up together" with the resurrected dead "to meet the Lord in the air: and *so shall we ever be with the Lord.*"

Don't miss that last part. Paul clarified that all true Christians—those who have previously died and those who are still living when Jesus returns—shall "ever be with the Lord" *when He returns,* not before.

Again, this is the Word of the living God.

In other words, we don't go "home to be with the Lord" at the moment of death, as so many ministers and priests mistakenly teach today. No, no, no. Again, we get to "be with the Lord" *when He descends from the sky.* Paul concluded his message by saying, "Therefore comfort one another with these words." Verse 18. This truth truly should "comfort" believers who have lost loved ones.

Paul's words in 1 Thessalonians 4:13–18 perfectly agree with the teaching of Jesus Christ Himself, who had previously told His disciples:

> "Let not your heart be troubled: You believe in God, believe also in Me. In My Father's house are many mansions; if it were not so, I would have told you. I go to prepare a place for you. And if I go and prepare a place for you, *I will come*

SATAN'S FIRST LIE

again and receive you to Myself; that where I am, there you may be also." John 14:1–3 (emphasis added).

In this well-known Bible passage, Jesus didn't tell His beloved disciples, "I'll meet you up in Heaven shortly after you die." Instead, He promised to "receive" His followers when He comes "again."

Years ago, I discussed this topic on the phone with a Christian pastor in New Mexico who firmly believed in the immortal soul theory, and in the subsequent theory that the souls of all believers fly to Heaven instantly when their physical bodies stop breathing. "How do you explain John 14:3?" I asked that pastor. "According to these words of Jesus," I continued, "when do believers go to be with Him? When they die? Or when He returns?"

The pastor's silence was deafening.

He had no answer.

Again, according to God's Word, believers who die have "fallen asleep" and simply continue to "sleep in Jesus." During this earthly life, while it may take a while to finally drift off to sleep at night, most people who are truly asleep have little or no awareness of the passage of time. Often, many hours later, an alarm goes off, and it's time to wake up.

The same is literally true when a person dies. A year may pass by, or five years, or a hundred years, or even thousands of years, yet the sleeper has no awareness of time passing. Then suddenly—and it will seem like an instant—God's mighty trumpet will blast and it will be Resurrection Day. Then it will be time to "ever be with the Lord"! So, for all practical purposes, for true believers, the moment of death is but a heartbeat away from seeing our loving Savior face to face.

What a moment of joy that will be! Not only that, but we will also be reunited with our believing loved ones who were separated from us by death, never more to part.

To summarize, according to God's Book, those who have died are sleeping quietly, peacefully, and painlessly awaiting the resurrection of the dead. Knowing this truth is not only enlightening and comforting, but it also protects us from being misled by malicious, heartless, demonic spirits that can easily personate dead people. Thus God's truth is both comforting and protecting.

On the other hand, if we don't know what the Bible plainly teaches about mortality, death, and evil spirits, we will be wide open to being hoodwinked by smooth-talking supernatural personalities claiming to be dead relatives, or deceased celebrities, or the virgin Mary, or one of Christ's apostles, or friendly aliens from distant galaxies, or someone else.

To put it bluntly, we're like unsuspecting sitting ducks just waiting to be shot by a skillful hunter.

Don't be Satan's victim.

Be victorious through faith in God's Word.

Chapter 7

The Resurrection Factor

The central pillars of the Christian faith are that Jesus Christ is "the Son of God" (John 20:31), that He sacrificed His life for "the sins of the whole world" upon a cross (1 John 2:2), and that He rose from the dead (1 Cor. 15:3, 4). On the day of His resurrection, a holy angel told Jesus' followers who had returned to His tomb, "Do not be afraid, for I know that you seek Jesus who was crucified. He is not here; for He is risen, as He said. Come, see the place where the Lord lay. And go quickly and tell His disciples that He is risen from the dead." Matt. 28:5–7.

Before His crucifixion, our Savior told His disciples that He "must go to Jerusalem, and suffer many things of the elders and chief priests and scribes, and be killed, and be raised again the third day." Matt. 16:21.

SATAN'S FIRST LIE

Although Christ predicted this numerous times, it was hard for His disciples to grasp these fundamental truths. And believe it or not, it is hard for many Christians today to grasp the implications of these same simple, basic truths.

The facts are these:

1. Jesus Christ died for our sins, rested in a grave, and rose from the dead.

2. Because of what Jesus did for us, when we die, we also will rest in graves, and later rise from the dead.

From a biblical perspective—to quote a common saying—points 1 and 2 are "as plain as the nose on your face." The Scriptures teach death, burial, and resurrection, not Satan's first lie that when sinners die, they don't really die; but instead, their supposedly immortal souls fly off into the Great Beyond. In the second half of this book, we will closely examine some other Bible verses that seem to teach natural soul immortality, but really don't. For now, let's focus more on the resurrection of the dead.

In John chapter 6, Jesus told a group of Jews:

"This is the will of the Father who sent Me, that of all He has given Me, I should lose nothing, but should raise it up at the last day." John 6:39 (emphasis added).

"And this is the will of Him who sent Me, that everyone who sees the Son and believes in Him may have everlasting life; and I will raise him up at the last day." Verse 40 (emphasis added).

"No one can come to Me unless the Father who sent Me draws him; and I will raise him up at the last day." Verse 44 (emphasis added).

"Whoever eats My flesh and drinks My blood has eternal life, and I will raise him up at the last day." Verse 54 (emphasis added).

Here Jesus Christ stated, not just once, or twice, or three times, but four times, that those who believe in Him will be resurrected after they die. When will they be resurrected? "At the last day." Thus Jesus Christ did not teach His followers that they will be with Him at the moment of their death, but "at the last day" when He returns at "the end of the world." Matt. 28:20.

To those who help others in this life, Jesus repeated: "You shall be repaid at the resurrection of the just." Luke 14:14. Thus true believers will be rewarded on Resurrection Day, not when they die.

Jesus Christ also taught that there will be two resurrections in the future, not just one. The Master Himself declared:

> "Do not marvel at this; for the hour is coming in which all who are in the graves will hear His voice and come forth—those who have done good, to the resurrection of life, and those who have done evil, to the resurrection of condemnation." John 5:28, 29.

Based on these words, then, where are dead people now? Our Savior's answer is clear: "in the graves." What will happen to these dead people in the future? Jesus said they will "hear His voice and come forth" from their dusty beds. Will everyone rise in the same resurrection? No. How many resurrections will there be? Two. What did the Truth Teller call these two different resurrections? He called them "the resurrection of life" and "the resurrection of condemnation."

Paul taught the same truths when he stated that "there will be a resurrection of the dead, both of the just and the unjust." Acts 24:15. Thus the teaching of two resurrections is firmly established in the New Testament.

"The resurrection of life" is the good resurrection of believers who awaken to "life" when Jesus Christ returns. This is when "the dead in Christ will rise first." 1 Thess. 4:16. The Book of Revelation states that "the resurrection of condemnation" takes place 1,000 years later on the great Day of Judgment (see Rev. 20:4–6, 11-15).

We will soon explore numerous other verses often quoted by well-meaning Bible-believing Christians—verses that seem at first glance to teach Satan's first lie, but which really don't. As you will soon discover, not only is the Devil a cruel and cunning foe, *but he even uses the Bible itself to promote his lies.*

Say a prayer.
Ask God for wisdom.
Then turn the page.

Chapter 8

Absent from the Body?

A close analysis of Satan's first lie—promoting the falsehood that sinners are naturally immortal—reveals that he was actually quoting God's own words; but he added one word of deception. God told Adam: If you sin, "you shall surely die." Gen. 2:17. Satan repeated God's exact words to Eve, but slyly tweaked them: "You will not surely die." Gen. 3:4. Thus the Devil quoted God's own words, but twisted them to lure Eve into sin.

In the New Testament, the master seducer adopted the same strategy. In Matthew 4:1–11, he tempted Jesus three times. Notice these details of Satan's second temptation:

> Then the Devil took Him up into the holy city, set Him on the pinnacle of the temple, and said to Him, "If You are the

Son of God, throw Yourself down. *For it is written:* 'He shall give His angels charge over you,' and, 'In their hands they shall bear you up, lest you dash your foot against a stone.' " Matt. 4:5, 6 (emphasis added).

Did you catch that? "It is written," *said the Devil.* From this we can learn three things: 1) Satan knows the Bible; 2) He will quote it; 3) He quotes it to deceive. In this case, the Devil quoted Psalm 91:11, 12, but he misused what was sacredly "written" to tempt Jesus to act contrary to God's will.

Notice Christ's response. "Jesus said to him, It is written *again* [emphasis added], 'You shall not tempt the LORD your God.' " Matt. 4:7.

When Satan tempted Jesus with "It is written," Christ replied with, "It is written again," to resist him. This teaches us two things: 1) We should know more than one Bible verse. 2) Sometimes we must use other Bible verses to defeat the Devil when he quotes isolated Bible verses in a false way.

As we have previously seen, many Bible verses teach that God "alone has immortality" (1 Tim. 6:16); that fallen humans are "mortal" (Job 4:17; Rom. 2:7; 1 Cor. 15:52); that when people die they are truly dead (Eccl. 9:5; Ps. 115:17) and sleep in their graves (Ps. 13:3; Dan. 12:2; John 11:11; Acts 7:60) until the resurrection (John 5:28, 29; 1 Thess. 4:16, 17).

But what about this next verse written by Paul? "We are confident, yes, well pleased rather to be absent from the body and to be present with the Lord." 2 Cor. 5:8.

Countless Christians quote this verse to prove that when we die we are *not* really dead, asleep, unconscious, and resting in our graves until the resurrection. Instead, our supposedly immortal souls exit this "body" and fly to Heaven to be "present with the Lord."

"It is written," many say, "that's what Paul wrote!"

Are they correct, or could Satan be cunningly using what was "written" by Paul to promote his first lie, just as he quoted some of God's own words to deceive Eve? To find out, we must look very closely at what Paul actually wrote (and didn't write), and also follow Christ's example of seeing what is "written *again*" in other places in order to get the full picture.

First, Paul was clearly writing about his own future transition away from his sinful "body" to being "present" with Jesus. But notice carefully that Paul doesn't say in that one verse exactly when this transition will occur. Most people assume he meant at the moment of death. But did he? Or did he mean on Resurrection Day when Jesus Christ returns?

"Jump!" Satan told Jesus in his second temptation, after quoting what was "written" in Psalm 91:11, 12. Before leaping to conclusions about what Paul really meant by his "absent from the body" statement, let's consider what was "written again" by Paul in other nearby verses.

Four verses earlier Paul had clarified that this transition occurs when "mortality" is "swallowed up by life." 2 Cor. 5:4. Here Paul clarified that "mortality" (not immortality) is our present state, but that someday we will become immortal. When? At death, or on Resurrection Day? If we back up a few chapters to Paul's first letter to the Corinthians, we find his answer.

> Behold, I show you a mystery: We shall not all *sleep*, but we shall all be changed, in a moment, in the twinkling of an eye, *at the last trump*: For the trumpet shall sound, and *the dead shall be raised incorruptible*, and we shall be changed. For this

corruptible must put on incorruption, and *this mortal must put on immortality.* So *when* this corruptibleshall have put on incorruption, and this mortal shall have put on immortality, *then* shall be brought to pass the saying that is written, Death is swallowed up in victory. O death, where is thy sting? O grave, where is thy victory? 1 Cor. 15:51–55, KJV (emphasis added).

Paul is describing the glorious return of Jesus Christ and the resurrection of God's saints. Looking closely, we see that Paul called death "sleep" (verse 51), again stated that we are now "mortal" (verse 53), and that it will be "at the last trump" when "the dead shall be raised . . . and we shall be changed" (verse 52). "*Then*," Paul clarified, "shall be brought to pass the saying that is written, *Death is swallowed up in victory.*" Verses 52-54 (emphasis added).

That last part about death being "swallowed up in victory" perfectly parallels what the apostle wrote in 2 Corinthians 5:4 about "mortality" being "swallowed up by life" which, four verses later, still further clarifies what Paul meant as he longed for that great future transition when he would finally be "absent" or eternally removed from his sinful "body," to be "present with the Lord." Putting these pieces together, we discover that it is when Jesus Christ returns that true believers will be with their Savior, not at the moment of death. Paul's words also parallel what he wrote to the Thessalonians:

> For the Lord Himself shall descend from Heaven with a shout, with the voice of the Archangel, and with the trump of God: and the dead in Christ shall rise first: Then we which are alive and remain shall be caught up together with them in the clouds, to meet the Lord in the air: *and so shall we ever be with the Lord.* 1 Thess. 4:16, 17 (emphasis added).

Putting all these verses together, Paul's meaning becomes as clear as sunlight. It is when Jesus Christ "descends from Heaven" with the sound of a mighty trumpet of God, that "the dead in Christ" (who died trusting the crucified and resurrected One) will rise from their dusty beds. *Then* those still living (I hope to be among this group) will be "caught up" to enjoy the greatest space ride humans have ever experienced!

On that fantastic day, all remnants of our

old sinful bodies will remain in the dust. We died "mortal," but will rise "immortal." And then? Don't miss it: "so shall we ever be with the Lord." This is the Word of God. Hallelujah!

In conclusion, by looking beyond one isolated verse, and by comparing it with "It is written *again*" (by looking at other verses), we can see that 2 Corinthians 5:8 does not teach Satan's first lie.

More to come . . .

CHAPTER 9

THE THIEF ON THE CROSS

We just saw how Satan has cunningly used Paul's own words in 2 Corinthians 5:8 to teach his first lie (that sinners don't really die), and now we will see how he can even use the words of Jesus Christ Himself to promote his delusions.

Follow closely. On history's darkest day, when God's own Son hung suspended between Heaven and Earth bearing the sins of the lost, a dying criminal crucified beside Jesus breathed hopefully, "Lord, remember me when You come into Your kingdom." Luke 23:42.

Invisible holy angels waited anxiously to hear Christ's reply. Finally, the King responded, "Assuredly, I say to you, today you will be with Me in Paradise." Luke 23:43. Many interpret Christ's response as conclusive

SATAN'S FIRST LIE

evidence that the dying thief's soul instantly flew into the glorious presence of Jesus on that very day.

But this is impossible.

Here's why:

First, notice the exact words of the dying thief. He pleaded, "Lord, remember me *when you come into Your kingdom.*" Thus the thief's plea was not to be remembered immediately, but in the future when Jesus would "come" into His kingdom—that is, at His Second Coming, not before.

Second, Jesus didn't enter Paradise that day. Instead, after He died, His body was gently placed into Joseph's tomb. Three days later, after rising from the dead, Jesus told Mary, "*I have not yet ascended to My Father.*" John 20:17 (emphasis added). These words prove that our Lord did not ascend to join either the crucified thief or His Heavenly Father in glory on the day of His death.

Third, the thief didn't even die that day. We know this because, at the setting of the sun the Roman soldiers broke his legs (see John 19:32) to prevent him from escaping during the next few days as he slowly died.

Finally, as we've already seen, Jesus stated that His followers will be with Him *when He returns.* "I will come again," He promised, "*and receive you to Myself.*" John 14:3 (emphasis added). Paul taught the same thing when he wrote that believers will "be with the Lord" only when He descends from Heaven and resurrects the dead (see 1 Thess. 4:16, 17). What then did Jesus mean when He spoke to the dying thief?

The confusion stems from the placement of one seemingly insignificant mark of punctuation, a comma. Before looking again at Christ's exact words to the thief, let me clarify that the Bible is the Word of God, not the Comma of God. It was only after the Bible was written that much of its punctuation and the numbering of verses was added by translators. Whatever translation you own, most Bibles insert "Chapter 23" before verse "42" which contains the request of the dying thief. Christ's answer is then found in verse "43."

But guess what? Luke (who wrote the book of Luke) didn't actually write "Chapter 23" or verse "42" et cetera. Instead, he wrote one continual book, without adding any chapters or verses. It wasn't until many years later that men numbered the verses to make it easier for us to find them. I'm glad they did, for it makes it much easier for us to look up verses

SATAN'S FIRST LIE

and study the Bible. But translators also added punctuation, which included inserting commas where they assumed they should go. So let's remove the comma—a human addition to the text—to see what Jesus literally said to the thief. As rendered in the New King James Version, His exact words in Luke 23:43 would then appear like this:

> "Assuredly I say to you today you will be with Me in Paradise."

If you place the comma before the word "today" (where most Bibles place it), then Jesus told the thief, "*Today* you will be with Me in Paradise." But if you place the comma *after* "today," Christ's meaning is changed entirely. Then Jesus would have said, "I say to you today, you will [future tense] be with Me in Paradise." In other words, Christ would be telling the thief, "Assuredly I say to you today (at this moment that I'm hanging on a cross) that you *will be with Me in the future when I return as King of kings and Lord of lords.*"

So which is it?

Where should the comma go?

Fortunately, we don't have to guess, because the other verses we already read make Christ's

THE THIEF ON THE CROSS

meaning clear. To summarize again: *First*, Jesus didn't enter Paradise that day. *Second*, on Sunday morning He had not yet ascended to His Father (see John 20:17). *Third*, the thief didn't die that day (it normally took three to four days for crucified criminals to die); and *fourth*, Jesus never contradicted Himself. He plainly promised His followers, "I will come again and receive you to Myself." John 14:3.

In the year 1521, a lone monk named Martin Luther stood before a large Roman Catholic council in Worms, Germany, to defend the new teachings he found in the Bible. After being relentlessly questioned and urged to follow common Catholic traditions, Luther finally took his stand on the Scriptures. "Here I stand," he bravely replied, "So help me God. Amen."

I stand on the same Word of God.

According to John 14:1–3; 1 Corinthians 15:51–55; and 1 Thessalonians 4:16–18, true believers in our wonderful Lord Jesus Christ will finally have the privilege of being with Him forever when He returns to gather His people.

Therefore, once again, I hope you can see that a correct understanding of "It is written" does *not* teach Satan's first lie.

CHAPTER 10

MOSES AND ELIJAH

Another New Testament passage that Satan uses to teach his immortal soul delusion is the one that describes the physical appearance of Moses and Elijah (who lived in Old Testament times) in front of our Savior not long before His terrible crucifixion.

The scene is recorded in Matthew 17:1–8 and starts out with Jesus, Peter, James, and John hiking up a mountain. When they reached the summit, Jesus was suddenly "transfigured before them. His face shone like the sun, and His clothes became as white as the light." Matt. 17:2. The Heavenly Father no doubt manifested His magnificent glory to encourage His Son before His terrible trial, and also to strengthen the faith of Christ's disciples that Jesus truly was the Sent of God.

Then, suddenly, "there appeared to them

MOSES AND ELIJAH

Moses and Elijah" (verse 3) who began conversing with the Savior. Many interpret the verse as proof that: 1) The dead are really alive on the Other Side, and 2) Talking to dead people is not only possible, but even advisable.

Actually, this Bible verse teaches no such thing, as you are about to discover.

First, it wasn't two disembodied souls or ghosts that appeared before Christ and His three disciples. Instead, it was "two men" (Luke 9:30) in physical form.

Second, Elijah never died in Old Testament times. Instead, he was literally translated or taken to Heaven in a cloudy chariot while his associate Elisha watched (see 2 Kings 2:11).

Third, yes, Moses did die, but the New Testament indicates that he was later resurrected back to life when Michael the Archangel came down from Heaven and "disputed with the Devil about the body of Moses." Jude 9. Satan was furious. "You can't have him!" he probably fumed. Michael didn't argue back, but simply replied, "The Lord rebuke you!" Thus the "body of Moses" was snatched from the grave, raised to life early, and then taken up to glory. Later, Elijah joined him after he was translated without seeing death. We can also assume that both Moses and Elijah met Enoch in Heaven who was also translated (see Gen. 5:24) before Noah's Flood.

On the Mount of Transfiguration, God sent Moses and Elijah down from Heaven to encourage His Son on Earth. To Jesus, who was now standing in the deepening shadows of His approaching death on a cross, Moses represented all those who would someday be resurrected when Christ returns, while Elijah represented those who would someday be translated without seeing death on that same glorious day.

Years later, the apostle Paul later described both groups (the resurrected and translated saints represented by Moses and Elijah) when he wrote:

> For the Lord Himself will descend from Heaven with a shout, with the voice of an Archangel, and with thetrumpet of God. And the dead in Christ will rise first. Then we who are alive and remain shall be caught up together with them in the clouds to meet the Lord in the air. And thus we shall always be with the Lord. 1 Thess. 4:16, 17.

MOSES AND ELIJAH

Significantly, right before Matthew 17:1–8 that mentions Moses and Elijah, Jesus told His disciples, "There are some standing here who shall not taste death till they see the Son of Man coming in His kingdom." Matt. 16:28. Six days later (see Matt. 17:1), Jesus took Peter, James, and John up the mountain where He was transfigured and Moses and Elijah appeared. In essence, those disciples then witnessed God's future kingdom in miniature. They saw Jesus (the King of glory) transfigured and Moses and Elijah representing all the future resurrected and translated saints.

Essentially, they saw the Kingdom of God!

May this revelation also inspire us to commit ourselves fully to Jesus Christ and His Word so we too can be "in that number, when the saints go marching in."

Chapter 11

Souls Under the Altar

In the last book of the Bible, we read:

> When He opened the fifth seal, I saw under the altar the souls of those who had been slain for the Word of God and for the testimony which they held. And they cried with a loud voice, saying, "How long, O Lord, holy and true, until You judge and avenge our blood on those who dwell on the Earth?" Then a white robe was given to each of them; and it was said to them that they should rest a little while longer, until both the number of their fellow servants and their brethren, who would be killed as they were, was completed. Rev. 6:9–11.

Here John "saw" under an "altar" in Heaven

"the souls" of many Christian martyrs crying for vengeance against their persecutors. "There!" many claim, "The Bible says that souls are alive in Heaven after they have died!"

Does this passage verify Satan's first sermon in the garden of Eden that we shall "not surely die"?

Absolutely not!

First, it seems obvious that Revelation chapter six contains much symbolism. For instance, earlier in the same chapter, John also saw four horses with four riders, the fourth rider being "Death" itself, followed by "Hell" (see Rev. 6:1–8). Can "Death" *literally* ride a horse? Can real souls somehow become crammed beneath a physical altar? Not a very pleasant place to hang out, wouldn't you agree?

Biblically speaking, the idea of martyred souls crying out for vengeance is rooted in Genesis 4 when God spoke to Cain after he cruelly murdered his brother Abel, saying, "What have you done? The voice of your brother's blood cries out to Me from the ground." Gen. 4:10. Does this mean that Abel's blood somehow literally uttered anguished complaints through dirt? No.

Again, this must be symbolic language.

SATAN'S FIRST LIE

The Book of Revelation is filled with imagery that shouldn't be taken literally, such as the rising of a seven-headed, ten-horned beast (see Rev. 13:1) or the appearance of a seductive harlot named Babylon who is "drunk with the blood of the saints." Rev. 17:4, 6. Yes, some parts of Revelation should be taken literally, such as the return of Jesus Christ when "every eye shall see Him." Rev. 1:7. But other parts are obviously symbolic. It is up to us, guided by the Holy Spirit, to discern the difference.

One thing's for sure: the idea of myriads of floating souls somehow being packed beneath a heavenly altar doesn't make sense. The point is that someday the Lord's just vengeance will be executed upon cruel murderers of His people. That day is surely coming. But not yet. Revelation 6:9–11 also tells us that Christian martyrs have *not yet* received their reward. Yet someday they will.

When will that be?

Jesus said that they "shall be repaid at the resurrection of the just." Luke 14:14.

CHAPTER 12

THE HOT TOPIC OF HELL

It's time to shift gears from death and the grave to the hot topic of hell. As can be expected, opinions differ widely about what hell really means. Some teach that it means nothing more than "separation from God." Others strongly disagree. "It's not just separation," they counter, "but a *fiery* separation where rejectors of God will writhe in eternal flames forever!" The traditional view is that hell is a hot, smoky place somewhere beneath our feet where lost souls instantly descend the moment they die. According to this frightening belief, the damned are sizzling somewhere right now, consciously, painfully.

Throughout Christian history, millions have been taught that hell never ends.

When I was 20 years old, a Christian pastor told me that hell is a dark place where those

SATAN'S FIRST LIE

who reject Jesus will be tortured forever. At that time, this concept was new to me, and it distressed me greatly. No one in my family believed in Jesus. I was especially close to my father, and when I first learned that he might suffer pain eternally, I went home and nearly cried my eyes out right in front of him.

As we begin to unravel this highly emotional subject, let me first clarify that I certainly believe what the *Bible* teaches about hell. So don't worry about that. I'm not a Scripture-rejecting heretic. Yet as we dive deeper into this controversial topic you will discover that what most people *think* about hell doesn't really line up with what God's Word *actually* says.

Above all, you will see that the biblical truth about hell does *not* support Satan's first lie. But don't take my word for anything. As always, I encourage you to pick up your own Bible and see for yourself what it really teaches.

In the New Testament, there are actually *three different Greek words* translated as "hell" in our English Bibles, and each word means something different. These three Greek words are:

1. *Tartarus*
2. *Gehenna*
3. *Hades*

Tartarus is used only once in the New Testament, in the book of 2 Peter. The Scripture reads:

> God spared not the angels that sinned, but cast them down to hell [Tartarus], and delivered them into chains of darkness, to be reserved unto Judgment. 2 Peter 2:4, KJV.

This verse says that "the angels that sinned" (which would obviously include Lucifer, their leader) have already been cast down "to hell" by God. Yet they aren't roasting right now, and they certainly aren't suffering somewhere beneath Los Angeles, Paris, or Tokyo. Instead, *Tartarus* is merely the temporary place where Satan and his evil angels currently abide. It isn't the place of final punishment, either. Look carefully. 2 Peter 2:4 clarifies that Satan and his wicked angels are "reserved *unto* Judgment" (KJV, emphasis added), which means that their full punishment is yet future. For Lucifer and his diabolical demons, the flames haven't been ignited yet.

So much for *Tartarus*.

Next word: *Gehenna*. Most credible authorities admit that this word is derived from the name of the narrow, rocky Valley of Hinnom just southwest of Jerusalem where trash, filth, and the bodies of dead animals were consumed by fire in Bible times. Jesus Christ plainly made use of the imagery of that ancient Jewish fire pit when He warned that those who keep sinning are in "danger of hell [*Gehenna*] fire." Matt. 5:22; see also verses 29, 30. Thus *Gehenna* does suggest real flames. But a key question is: *When* do those fires burn?

In Matthew 13:24–30, Jesus told a striking parable about a farmer, wheat, weeds, reapers, and a harvest. A little later, He explained its meaning:

> The harvest is the end of the world, and the reapers are the angels. As therefore *the tares [weeds] are gathered and burned in the fire; so shall it be at the end of this world.* The Son of Man shall send forth His angels, and they shall gather out of His kingdom all things that offend, and them which do iniquity; and shall cast them into a furnace of fire: there shall be wailing and gnashing of teeth. Then shall the righteous shine forth as the sun in the kingdom of their Father. Who hath ears to hear, let him hear. Matt. 13:39–43, KJV (emphasis added).

As to *when* the fire burns, Christ's direct explanation in verse 40 was: "So shall it be at the end of this world." In other words, that fire is *not* burning now. Peter affirmed the same thing when he wrote:

> But the heavens and the Earth, which are now, by the same word are kept in store, *reserved unto fire against the Day of Judgment and perdition of ungodly men.* 2 Peter 3:7, KJV (emphasis added).

Peter's words reveal these five facts:

1. A real fire is coming.

2. It will burn "the heavens," which means the expanse of space above, including the polluted atmosphere we breathe.

3. It will burn "the Earth," the very planet we earthlings daily tread.

4. It will blaze on "the Day of Judgment."

5. "Ungodly men" will end up in this fire.

A few verses later, Peter elaborated further:

> But the Day of the Lord will come as a thief in the night; in the which the heavens shall pass away with a great noise, and the elements shall melt with fervent heat, the Earth also and the works that are therein shall be burned up. 2 Peter 3:10, KJV.

This passage is simple and straightforward. At some point *in the future* the sky above us and the earth beneath our feet will literally ignite and "melt with fervent heat." So if you've been taught that the sum total of hellfire is some smoky place miles beneath our feet, think again. The Bible says our entire sin-polluted planet is destined for flames. But there's good news, too. Peter concluded with this comforting assurance:

> Nevertheless we, according to His promise, look for new heavens and a New Earth, in which righteousness dwells. 2 Peter 3:13.

These enlightening verses teach that God will use real flames to cleanse this present sin-polluted Earth of its decay and wickedness, but then He will marvelously recreate it entirely. This is "His promise" to which "we" should be looking earnestly forward.

The Book of Revelation teaches the same message about the final resurrection of the lost, a great Judgment Day, followed by cleansing fire, followed by a new heaven and earth. Look carefully at this solemn, inspired sequence:

> The rest of the dead [who missed the first resurrection when Jesus returns] did not live again until the thousand years were finished. . . . I saw a great white throne and Him who sat on it. . . . And I saw the dead, small and great, standing before God [after the second resurrection], and books were opened. And another book was opened, which is the Book of Life. And the dead [who were just raised] were judged according to their works, by the things which were written in the books. . . . Then Death and Hades were cast into the lake of fire. This is the second death. And anyone not found written in the Book of Life was cast into the lake of fire. Now I saw a new heaven and a New Earth, for the first heaven and the first Earth had passed away. . . . Then He who sat on the throne said, "Behold, I make all things new." And He said to me, "Write, for

these words are true and faithful." Rev. 20:5, 11–15; 21:1, 5.

Here's the inspired sequence:

1. At the end of the thousand years, the lost are raised back to life. This is the second resurrection.

2. Then they stand before God's "great white throne" for His just judgment.

3. They are judged fairly, "according to their works."

4. They will then be punished in "the lake of fire."

5. Finally, God will create "a new heaven and a New Earth." Obviously, He will not obliterate holy, sinless Heaven, but only our polluted heavens or atmosphere.

Thus our Lord Jesus Christ, His disciple Peter, and the last book of the Bible all teach that real fire is coming "at the end of this world." This fire will not only be the location in which those who reject God will be punished, but it will serve a dual function of purifying our smog-polluted skies and chemically-saturated ground from every vestige of impurity. Then the just Judge will marvelously recreate a new atmospheric heaven and a pristine Earth to become the eternal home of those who have repented of their sins and trusted fully in what our merciful Savior did for us all on His cross.

One sober fact is that "all liars" will eventually wind up "in the lake which burns with fire and brimstone, which is the second death." Rev. 21:8. This should impress us with the importance of knowing and speaking the truth, which includes rejecting Satan's first lie.

The third Greek word for hell is *Hades*. Some English Bibles translate it as hell, while others, like the New International Version, leave the word "Hades" unchanged. Now here's a key point: In Revelation 20:14, "Hades" is finally "cast *into* the lake of fire." Thus "Hades" is not the dreaded fiery place, but itself is cast into a fiery place.

Here is the verse in both the KJV and NIV:

> And death and *hell* were cast into the lake of fire. Rev. 20:14, KJV (emphasis added).

SATAN'S FIRST LIE

Then death and *Hades* were thrown into the lake of fire. Rev. 20:14, NIV (emphasis added).

In my personal King James Version, a marginal note beside the word "hell" (Hades) in Revelation 20:14 states that *Hades* literally means "*the grave*." Thus Revelation 20:14 could properly be translated, "death and *the grave* were cast into the lake of fire."

To make it simple, "Hades" literally means "the grave." This is easy to prove from 1 Corinthians 15:55, which in the King James Version states,

O death, where is thy sting? O grave [Hades], where is thy victory? 1 Cor. 15:55, KJV (emphasis added).

If you look in any Strong's Concordance, you'll discover that the original Greek word here translated "grave" is "Hades." By looking at the context, it's obvious that "Hades" means "the grave" because *God's saints* rise from "Hades" when Jesus Christ returns. See for yourself:

Behold, I show you a mystery; we shall

not all sleep, but we shall all be changed, in a moment, in the twinkling of an eye, at the last trump: for the trumpet shall sound, and the dead shall be raised incorruptible, and we shall be changed. For this corruptible must put on incorruption, and this mortal must put on immortality. So when this corruptible shall have put on incorruption, and this mortal shall have put on immortality, then shall be brought to pass the saying that is written, Death is swallowed up on victory. Odeath, where is thy sting? *O grave* [Hades] *where is thy victory*? 1 Cor. 15:51–55, KJV (emphasis added).

"O grave [Hades], where is your victory?" God's resurrected saints triumphantly shout when Jesus returns. Thus "Hades" *cannot* mean a place of burning, for who can imagine God's people writhing in flames as they await their glorious resurrection?

Impossible!

Additional proof that "Hades" means "the grave" is that "Hades" was the place Jesus Christ's body rested immediately after His death. In Acts 2:31, the King James Version declares,

His [Christ's] soul was not left *in hell* [Hades], neither [did] his flesh see corruption. Acts 2:31, KJV (emphasis added).

The New International Version puts it this way,

He [Christ] was not abandoned to *the grave,* nor did His body see decay. Acts 2:31 (emphasis added).

Thus Christ's "body" (NIV) or "flesh" (KJV) didn't see "corruption" (KJV) or "decay" (NIV) *because He rested in the tomb for only a short time before His resurrection.*

To summarize the meaning of the three Greek words translated "Hell" in our English Bibles:

1. *Tartarus* (see 2 Peter 2:4) is the place where Satan and his wicked angels now await their future punishment.

2. *Gehenna* means a place of fire, brimstone, and punishment (see Matt. 5:22, 29, 30, described in Matt. 13:40–42 & 2 Peter 3:7,10-12). These flames are yet future, "at the end of the world."

3. *Hades* means "the grave" (see Acts 2:31; 1 Cor. 15:55; Rev. 20:14). Jesus Christ's body rested there, and His saints are resting there now until Resurrection Day.

In its description of this final fire, and the doom of the lost, the Bible's last book solemnly declares, "Whosoever was not found written in the Book of Life was cast into the lake of fire." Rev. 20:15, KJV.

The next question to consider is *how long* this final "lake of fire" will burn. Will it burn forever, or will its ill-fated inhabitants, including Satan and his wicked demons, completely *burn up,* and thus cease to exist altogether?

What does God's Word really say?

Chapter 13

Will Hellfire Burn Forever?

Will *Gehenna*—the word the New Testament uses in reference to the future punishment of lost people in hellfire—burn forever, and ever, and ever, and ever, or will its red-hot flames finally be extinguished? To discover the correct answer to this momentous question, we must accept what the Bible teaches above the opinions of men. As we keep exploring this controversial topic, let me again make my personal position clear.

I believe God's Word above popular theories.

That said, first of all, this subject requires close scrutiny, for some Bible texts do appear (like others we have looked at) to actually support Satan's first lie that those who disobey God "shall not surely die" (see Gen. 3:4). But, consistent with what we have discovered throughout this book, *such verses really don't teach that lost sinners will exist endlessly beyond their brief mortal life.*

For instance, in Matthew 25:41, Jesus warned that unsaved sinners will be plunged "into the everlasting fire prepared for the Devil and his angels." "That settles it for me!" many conclude, "The lost will sizzle eternally—and don't even try to convince me otherwise!" But consider that our Savior also declared that "God so loved the world, that He gave His only begotten Son, that whosoever believes in Him should *not perish*, but have eternal life." John 3:16 (emphasis added).

So which is it? Will the damned roast eternally in "everlasting fire," or finally "perish" and thus cease to exist?

Another example of apparent contradiction concerns the fate of Lucifer. The Book of Revelation says that "the Devil" will "be tormented day and night forever" in the lake of fire (see Rev. 20:10). "There's more proof!" some contend, "Satan will never cease frying like an egg in God's retributive skillet!"

Yet Ezekiel chapter 28 reveals a different picture. Initially discussing the ancient "king of Tyre" (verse 12), God's prophet then looks behind the scenes and identifies Lucifer, "the anointed cherub" (verse 14), who once inhabited "Eden, the garden of God" (verse 13), and who was originally "perfect in [his] ways from the day [he] was created," until "iniquity was found in [him]" (verse 15). Predicting this rebellious angel's final fate, God declares:

> ... therefore will I bring forth a fire from the midst of thee, *it shall devour thee, and I will bring thee to ashes* upon the earth in the sight of all them that behold thee. ... thou shalt be a terror, and *never shalt thou be anymore.* Ezek. 28:18, 19, KJV (emphasis added).

Again, which is it? Will the Devil be "tormented day and night" throughout endless ages, or become "ashes" and "never be anymore"?

The Bible doesn't contradict itself. These are only *apparent* contradictions. The solution to this dilemma is to continue doing what we have been doing by closely examining not only what "is written" (remembering that Satan often quotes Scripture falsely), but also what "is written *again.*" Matt. 4:7 (emphasis added). In other words, we must look at what the entire Bible says about any topic. When we look at the big picture—by comparing Scripture with Scripture—we will discover that everything fits and makes perfect sense.

Looking forward to the great "Day of the Lord," God Himself declares:

> "For behold, the day is coming, burning like an oven, and all the proud, yes, all who do wickedly will be *stubble*. And the day which is coming shall *burn them up*," says the LORD of hosts, "*that will leave them neither root nor branch*. . . . You shall trample the wicked, for *they shall be ashes* under the soles of your feet on the day that I do this," says the LORD of hosts." Malachi 4:1, 3 (emphasis added).

Here "the Lord of hosts" is speaking, not man. When His Day of Judgment finally bursts upon "those who do wickedly," He says it will "*burn them up*" and reduce them to "ashes," so that "neither root nor branch" remains. Think about it. If "neither root nor branch" of a plant remains, how much is left? *Nothing.*

This is what God says will happen to the wicked. The Psalmist David concurred:

SATAN'S FIRST LIE

As wax melts before the fire, so let the wicked *perish* at the presence of God. Ps. 68:2 (emphasis added).

For yet a little while and *the wicked shall be no more.*" Ps. 37:10 (emphasis added).

The enemies of the LORD, like the splendor of the meadows, shall vanish. *Into smoke they shall vanish away.* Ps. 37:20 (emphasis added).

But the transgressors shall be *destroyed together;* the future of the wicked shall be cut off. Ps. 37:38 (emphasis added).

John the Baptist also prophesied this about Jesus: "He will *burn u*p the chaff with unquenchable fire." Matt. 3:12 (emphasis added).

Concerning those who "obey not the Gospel," Paul wrote: "These shall be punished with *everlasting destruction.*" 2 Thess. 1:9 (emphasis added).

Paul also declared: "*The wages of sin is death,* but the gift of God is eternal life through Jesus Christ our Lord." Rom. 6:23 (emphasis added).

WILL HELLFIRE BURN FOREVER?

Years ago I presented these passages during a Bible seminar I held in Woodbury, New Jersey. In the audience, a Jewish man named Corrie listened with rapt attention. Very carefully I built my case that a loving God will administer nothing more than fair justice on Judgment Day, and that this will result in the tragic, total annihilation of those who have rejected His free gift of salvation through His Son, Jesus Christ. At the end of my talk, with tear-filled eyes, Corrie approached me with an outstretched hand. "Steve, now I can believe in God's love!" He then admitted that the idea of God torturing unsaved sinners forever—including his Jewish mother—had always prevented him from having personal faith in Jesus Christ.

Then Corrie walked away.

The next night I spoke again before the same crowd about the same topic. When I finished, Corrie once again approached me, but this time his face was glowing. "Last night," he excitedly reported, "I went home, dropped to my knees, and accepted Jesus as my Savior. Praise God!" Then happily announced, "I'm born again!" Corrie was baptized at the conclusion of my seminar. His mother came. "I don't know what's happened to my son," she said, "but he's so happy. What more can a mother want?"

In Corrie's case, the doctrine that God would someday banish sinners to an eternally burning location called "Hell" had hindered him from becoming a Christian. During my seminar, the true teaching of the Bible finally burst upon his misguided mind like a bright sunbeam from Heaven. Now he was a believer in Jesus Christ and was baptized.

Was Corrie deceived (by me), or had he at last discovered that Satan's first lie (that those who disobey God will "not surely die") was just that . . . a big fat lie!

Let's dig deeper and find out.

CHAPTER 14

ETERNAL FLAMES EXTINGUISHED

I once heard a story about how the late famous boxer, Mohammed Ali boarded an airplane but refused to buckle up. "Mr. Ali," commanded the flight attendant, "everyone must fasten their seatbelt." "I don't need a seatbelt," the fighter proudly responded, "I'm Superman!" "No, you're not," the woman countered promptly, "Superman didn't need an airplane. Now fasten your seatbelt or you will be ushered off this aircraft!" Needless to say, the muscular man with a powerful punch finally complied with the demand of a much smaller woman.

The moral of this story is that each of us—including famous people—needs a healthy dose of humility. Jesus said, "Everyone who exalts himself will be humbled, and he who humbles himself will be exalted." Luke 18:14.

SATAN'S FIRST LIE

As we continue our quest to correctly comprehend the doctrine of hellfire, it is my hope that each of my readers will put aside preconceived opinions and *humbly examine the Bible texts below.*

First, let's take a close look at the single-chapter book of Jude, right before Revelation. At the beginning of his letter, Jude urged Christians to "earnestly contend for the faith which was once delivered to the saints." Verse 3. Next he warned of "certain men" who were planting false doctrines inside the early church (see verse 4). In verses 5 and 6, Jude warned of the consequences of being led astray. Then he warned about "the vengeance of eternal fire." Verse 7.

Here's the entire verse:

> Even as Sodom and Gomorrah, and the cities about them in like manner, giving themselves over to fornication, and going after strange flesh, are set forth for an example, suffering the vengeance of eternal fire. Jude 7.

Notice carefully that it was the physical cities of Sodom and Gomorrah that "suffered the vengeance of eternal fire," not just their

Eternal Flames Extinguished

notoriously wicked inhabitants. In addition, the punishment that fell upon both the people, their gardens, orchards, streets, and buildings has been "set forth as an example" of what will happen to the unsaved. Writing an almost identical verse, Peter inserted one tiny, yet super-significant detail. Look closely:

> Turning the cities of Sodom and Gomorrah into ashes [God justly] condemned them with an overthrow, making them an ensample [example] unto all those that after should live ungodly. 2 Peter 2:6, KJV (emphasis added).

Putting Jude 7 alongside 2 Peter 2:6, we discover that the net result of that "eternal fire" which fell upon "the cities of Sodom and Gomorrah" turned them into ashes. But that's not all. Describing "the punishment of the sin of Sodom," the prophet Jeremiah included yet another critical detail by stating that those infamously evil cities were "overthrown as *in a moment.*" Lamentations 4:6 (emphasis added).

By piecing Jude 7, 2 Peter 2:6, and Lamentations 4:6 together, we discover that "the vengeance of eternal fire" was so searingly hot that it reduced Sodom, Gomorrah, a few other surrounding cities, and all of their inhabitants "into ashes" in "a moment" of time.

Again, think about it. Are Sodom, Gomorrah, and those other cities still destroyed? Yes indeed. Are they burning today? Obviously not. Then what does "eternal fire" mean *biblically?* By comparing Scripture with Scripture, it means that the fire originated with God and that *the punishment* lasts forever, *but not the flames.* Not only that, but both Jude and Peter called this punishment "an example" of what will someday overwhelm every wicked city and lost soul that finally and fully rejects God's love.

Jesus Christ also warned that He will someday sadly declare to every lost sinner, "Depart from Me, you cursed, into the *everlasting fire* prepared for the Devil and his angels." Matt. 25:41 (emphasis added). Will this "everlasting fire" be the same type of "eternal fire" mentioned in Jude 7 that destroyed Sodom and Gomorrah completely? Yes, because five verses later our Savior clarified, "And these [the lost] will go away into everlasting punishment, but the righteous into life eternal." Matt. 25:46. Thus this final "everlasting fire" will be just like the "eternal fire" that fell upon the Sodomites because it will result in "everlasting punish*ment*," not unceasing punish*ing*.

In other words, Jeremiah, Jesus, Peter, and Jude all agree that it is the punishment, not the punishing, that lasts forever.

Similarly, Paul also wrote about the "everlasting" consequences that will overwhelm all unsaved sinners when our Lord Jesus Christ returns "*in flaming fire* taking vengeance on them that know not God, and that obey not the Gospel of our Lord Jesus Christ: who shall be *punished with everlasting destruction* from the presence of the Lord, and from the glory of His power." 2 Thess. 1:8, 9 (emphasis added). Here the word *everlasting* is coupled with the word destruction—which means that the lost will be utterly destroyed forever, just like the cities of Sodom and Gomorrah.

In addition to Jeremiah, Jesus Christ, Peter, Jude, and Paul, John the Baptist also warned about "unquenchable fire" engulfing all rejectors of God. On the surface, one might assume John meant endless flames. But he didn't. Calling the saved "wheat" and the lost "chaff," the wilderness prophet announced that God's Messiah would "throughly [thoroughly] purge His floor, and gather His wheat into the garner; but He will *burn up the chaff*

SATAN'S FIRST LIE

with unquenchable fire." Matt. 3:12 (emphasis added). Thus the phrase, "unquenchable fire," doesn't mean its flames burn forever, but rather that its raging fire can't be snuffed out by man.

It will "*burn up the chaff,*" the Baptist warned, until nothing is left.

The 110-story Twin Towers of the World Trade Center in New York City no longer exist. On September 11, 2001, they were horrifically torpedoed by two hijacked planes on a mission of death. When the airplanes crashed into those towers, their jet fuel tanks ignited and the resultant blazing fires could not be quenched. Today, only their memories remain. For those who lost loved ones in New York City, the results of that fateful day seem eternal. In a similar but far more stupendous and widespread fashion, unquenchable fires obliterated Sodom and Gomorrah.

Tragically, the Muslim terrorists who brought down the Twin Towers believed they were serving Allah (their God). They also imagined they would soon be rewarded with 72 virgins in Heaven for their faithfulness to God's truth. But they were wrong. On Judgment Day, they will discover that their future will be quite different from their expectations.

Eternal Flames Extinguished

How about us?

We can't afford to make any serious mistakes about our future destinies. But if we stick closely to God's Word, we'll have no regrets.

CHAPTER 15

WORMS IN UNQUENCHABLE FIRE

Our compassionate Savior solemnly warned that those who continue in sin will someday risk being "cast into hell, into the fire that shall never be quenched—where 'Their worm does not die, and the fire is not quenched.' " Mark 9:45, 46. Once again (which shouldn't surprise us by now), what is "written" in Mark 9 is often used to support Satan's first lie that sinners "will not surely die" but will live forever in a place of eternal torment. But, as we have so often seen, and will see once again, *a true understanding of God's Word doesn't teach this at all.*

First, a literal reading of the text doesn't exactly say that lost people won't die in the fire, but rather it is "*their worm*" that "does not die." Was Jesus saying that slimy worms will live eternally? Consider this: We know that Jesus sometimes used symbolic language. For instance, He once told a group of Jewish people that they must eat His flesh and drink His blood (see John 6:56); but He didn't mean that literally. Instead, He wanted them to receive His life-giving words into their souls (see verse 63).

In that ancient literal Gehenna fire pit southwest of Jerusalem, worms and maggots often feasted on the unburnt flesh of dead dogs and executed criminals. Those gross, wiggling creatures were always there. In Mark 9:42–48, our Savior was actually quoting Isaiah 66:24, the context of which makes His meaning clear. See for yourself:

> They [God's saved people] shall go forth and look upon *the carcasses of the men who have transgressed against Me:* for their worm shall not die, neither shall their fire be quenched; and they shall be an abhorring unto all flesh. Isa. 66:24, KJV (emphasis added).

Isaiah's prophecy, which Jesus quoted in Mark 9:42–48, warns about worms feasting on "the carcasses of the men" who kept breaking God's law, while the righteous (untouched by the flames) merely "look" upon this morbid scene. This prophecy applies to the

SATAN'S FIRST LIE

Day of Judgment when God's saved people will sadly behold *the dead bodies* of those who persistently rejected the Lord.

What about "the fire" that can't be "quenched"? In Jeremiah 17:27, God also warned ancient Israel that if they didn't repent, an "unquenchable fire" would burn up the city of Jerusalem. In that case, "unquenchable" simply meant it could not be quenched by humans, no matter how hard they tried. This literally happened in 586 B.C. when Jerusalem was burned to the ground by invading Babylonian armies (see 2 Kings 25:8–12). Similarly, when literal fire rained down from Heaven upon Sodom and Gomorrah, it was also unquenchable by man.

Yet, when all combustible material was finally consumed, those flames *went out*.

It will be the same when the lost receive their final punishment in "the lake of fire. *This is the second death.*" Rev. 20:14 (emphasis added). Unlike the first death we all experience, "the second death" has no resurrection. In other words, at the end of the thousand years, when the lost are raised back to life to receive their just judgment in the lake of fire, when they die a "second" time, they will vanish for good.

But what about when the Book of

Revelation says, "The smoke of their torment ascends up forever and ever" (14:11), the "smoke rose up forever" (19:3), and that "the Devil" will be "tormented day and night forever" (20:10)? "What about those verses, Mr. Wohlberg?" some may ask. "Don't they prove that the lost burn forever?"

No, they don't.

Once again, "that old serpent, called the Devil, and Satan" (Rev. 12:9, KJV) insidiously uses Scripture to teach his first lie.

Here's the key part. If you look closely at each "tormented forever" text in Revelation, *every one* has symbolism in it. Revelation 14:11 and 20:10 both refer to "the beast"; and Revelation 19:3 states, "*Her* smoke rose up forever." Whose smoke? *The whore riding the beast.* Will a *literal* seven-headed beast and a *literal* prostitute named "MYSTERY, BABYLON" *literally* sizzle forever?

Obviously not.

Again, *this is symbolism.*

Here's another key part: While Revelation 20:10 refers to the "beast" (a symbolic term), the false prophet, and the Devil all being tormented forever, the verse right before it says the opposite and contains no symbolism. See for yourself:

Verse 9: They [the resurrected lost] went up on the breadth of the earth [at the end of the 1,000 years], and compassed the camp of the saints about, and the beloved city [the New Jerusalem]: and fire came down from God out of Heaven, and *devoured them* (KJV; emphasis added).

Verse 10: And the Devil that deceived them was cast into the lake of fire and brimstone, where the *beast* and the false prophet are, and shall be tormented day and night forever and ever (KJV; emphasis added).

So which is it? The literal truth lies in the text that contains *no symbolism*: "fire came down . . . and devoured them." Verse 9. Beyond this, after "the lake of fire" is again described in verse 15, the next verse says, "I saw a new heaven and a New Earth: for the first heaven and the first Earth were passed away. Rev. 21:1 (emphasis added).

Revelation 20:9 says the unsaved are on "the Earth" when God's fire "devoured them." Thus "the Earth" is the location of "the lake of fire." After the lost are consumed in "the lake of fire," the very next verse says that the "first Earth" had "passed away," which must include the lake of fire. Then God will make "a new heaven and a New Earth" where there will be "no more death, neither sorrow, nor crying, neither shall there be any more pain: for the former things are passed away." Rev. 21:4, KJV.

Think seriously with me. If the lake of fire burns forever, and if lost people suffer there for all eternity, then Revelation 21:4 can never come true because there will always be—somewhere in God's universe—a dark place where miserable people are sorrowing, screaming, crying, and suffering pain forever.

But Revelation 21:4 says it will not be so because all those awful "former things"— which are the sad result of sin—will have "passed away."

What will remain?

Only love, happiness, peace, and joy.

I definitely want to be there, don't you?

CHAPTER 16

THE RICH MAN AND LAZARUS

My mom is dead. She was Jewish, and she didn't believe in Jesus. The same can be said of most of my Jewish relatives. According to countless well-meaning Christian teachers, unbelievers who die without accepting Jesus are doomed to suffer in eternal flames.

This book has made it abundantly clear that this popular teaching is actually based on Satan's first lie that those who sin will never die because they have immortal souls. Instead, as we have seen, we humans are now mortal (see Rom. 2:7, etc.), and those who persistently reject God will someday cease to exist (see Ps. 37:10, 38). Because of their sinful choices, their persistent rejection of God's love and grace, and their firm refusal to repent, they have forfeited eternal life. On Judgment Day, after being raised to life in

The Rich Man and Lazarus

"the resurrection of condemnation" (John 5:29), the only thing our just God can do is to pronounce a just sentence and then sadly pull the plug to permanently end their brief, sin-saturated existence.

I pray that my family members (and every reader of this book) will wake up before it's too late.

But there is one more Bible passage we haven't looked at yet that is now being quoted worldwide to teach *Satan's first lie*, that must be explained. I call it The Mother of All Misunderstood Hell Verses. It is the Story of the Rich Man and Lazarus.

Jesus Christ declared:

> There was a certain rich man who was clothed in purple and fine linen and fared sumptuously every day. But there was a certain beggar named Lazarus, full of sores, who was laid at his gate, desiring to be fed with the crumbs which fell from the rich man's table. Moreover the dogs came and licked his sores. So it was that the beggar died, and was carried by the angels to Abraham's bosom. The rich man also died and was buried. And being in torments in Hades, he lifted up his eyes

and saw Abraham afar off, and Lazarus in his bosom. Then he cried and said, "Father Abraham, have mercy on me, and send Lazarus that he may dip the tip of his finger in water and cool my tongue; for I am tormented in this flame." Luke 16:19–24.

After denying the rich man's request for a drop of water to cool his tongue, Abraham finally said, "If they do not hear Moses and the prophets, neither will they be persuaded though one rise from the dead." Verse 31.

To begin with, here's a monumental megapoint that cannot be overemphasized: This is the ONLY place in the entire New Testament that says that a lost soul descends into a fiery hell immediately at death. Such a doctrine isn't taught anywhere else—not by Matthew, Mark, John, James, Peter, or Jude. Nor by Paul, *not even once.*

Let that sink into your soul.

Second, as we have already seen, Jesus sometimes used symbolic language to illustrate deep spiritual truths, such as when He referred to Himself as a "temple" (John 2:19–21), "the Bread of Life" (John 6:35), "the Light of the world" (John 8:12), and

The Rich Man and Lazarus

His followers as "sheep" (John 10:28). He also told parables. Although His parables contain practical lessons, not every point should be taken literally. Is His story of the rich man and Lazarus a parable, too? Here are seven reasons why it is.

1. Jesus often began His parables with the phrase, "A certain man," or "A certain rich man," etc. (see Luke 14:16; 15:11; 16:1; 19:11, 12; 20:9, KJV). Because the story of the rich man and Lazarus begins with "There was a certain rich man," it's logical to assume that this story is also a parable.

2. A man *cannot* literally enter into "the bosom" or chest of another person as this parable describes.

3. Someone burning in real flames *cannot* carry on a normal conversation.

4. Those in hell and those in Heaven *cannot* directly communicate with each other, either.

5. Jesus represented the rich man as being

SATAN'S FIRST LIE

bodily in hell, with eyes, a mouth, and a tongue. This is obviously symbolic. If you were to dig up an actual dead rich man's grave, wouldn't his body be there? Of course, just like any other dead person's body.

6. An actual burning man would not request a little water to cool just his tongue. What about the rest of his body?

7. The rest of the Bible teaches that when real people die, *they are dead* (see John 11:14), lie *"silent in the grave"* (Ps. 31:17), and "know nothing" (Eccl. 9:5) until the time of "the resurrection of the dead." Acts 24:15.

Jesus didn't interpret every parable He told. Yet when His disciples asked Him to explain the one about a farmer, wheat, weeds, and a harvest, He stated plainly that real hellfire occurs at *the end of this world*, not at the moment of death (see Matt. 13:36–40).

The immediate context of Christ's parable about the rich man and Lazarus shows He was talking to wealthy Pharisees who were mocking Him with their tongues (see Luke

16:14). Those bigoted Pharisees believed the rich were blessed, while the poor were under God's curse. In His parable spoken directly *to them*, Jesus flipped things upside down by describing a saved poor man, and a lost rich man. The part about the rich man asking for his tongue to be soothed was a direct warning to those misguided men that their own lips were propelling them toward hellfire. Finally, at the end of His parable, Jesus declared that even resurrecting Lazarus from the dead wouldn't convince the doubters.

"If this is a parable," some may ask, "why did Jesus specify the name Lazarus, who was a real person?" (see John 11:1). A reasonable answer is because Christ's parable was also a prophecy. Not long after Jesus told this parable, He did resurrect a real person named Lazarus (see John 11:1–53); yet this mighty miracle still didn't convince those stubborn Pharisees that He was Israel's true Messiah (see John 11:46–53).

Here's a solid principle: We should interpret parables by the rest of the Bible, rather than the rest of the Bible in the light of one parable.

And again, the rest of the Bible is unmistakably clear: The dead *are dead* (John 11:14)

SATAN'S FIRST LIE

and are sleeping unconsciously in their graves (Psalms 13:3; 115:17, 146:4; Acts 7:30) until they are resurrected (Dan. 12:3; John 5:29).

The bottom line is: Don't let the Devil twist the meaning of Jesus Christ's story about a rich man and poor Lazarus to deceive you with *his first lie.*

CHAPTER 17

GOD'S INFINITE LOVE REVEALED

To nearby residents, it will always be remembered as "the Esperanza Fire." Deliberately ignited by an evil arsonist, the October 2006 wind-driven blaze destroyed nearly 60,000 acres and 34 homes 100 miles east of Los Angeles, California. Worst of all, it cost the lives of five brave firefighters who were suddenly engulfed in flames when the wind unexpectedly shifted.

On Sunday, November 5, nearly 10,000 mourners attended a memorial service for those five fallen heroes at an outdoor amphitheater in San Bernardino. "We will never forget their sacrifice," Governor Arnold Schwarzenegger eulogized. As the ceremony concluded, U.S. Forest Service airplanes soared overhead as bagpipers played "Amazing Grace."

As awful as the Esperanza Fire was, it bears

no comparison to the all-consuming "lake of fire" (Rev. 20:15) that the Bible predicts will finally incinerate those who have rejected God "at the end of the world." Matt. 13:40. In that California blaze, five brave firefighters tragically lost their physical lives. But what is that compared to the countless lost sinners "whose number is as the sand of the sea" (Rev. 20:8) who will meet their tragic, permanent, everlasting demise in the unquenchable apocalyptic furnace?

> Then Death and Hades were cast into the lake of fire. *This is the second death.* Rev. 20:14, 15.

> The cowardly, unbelieving, abominable, murderers, sexually immoral, sorcerers, idolaters, and all liars shall have their part in the lake which burns with fire and brimstone, *which is the second death.* Rev. 21:8.

Here we see that the Book of Revelation states twice that the final fate of lost sinners who will be "cast into the lake of fire" is "*the second death.*" Underscore that last word: *death.* One purpose of this book is to prove, contrary to popular opinion, that the final fate of the unsaved is not endless eternal pain, but "death." Rom. 6:23. They will "perish" (John 3:16) and become "ashes" (Mal. 4:3). As it is written: " 'The day which is coming shall burn them up,' says the LORD of hosts, 'that will leave them neither root nor branch.' " Mal. 4:1 (emphasis added).

This is God's Word, not man's opinion.

But I have saved my best argument for last. Every true Bible-believing Christian understands that on a cruel cross just outside Jerusalem, our Lord and Savior Jesus Christ paid the full price for the sins of the world. Agreed?

The Bible says unequivocally: "Christ died for *our sins*." 1 Cor. 15:3 (emphasis added). "He Himself is the propitiation [sacrifice] *for our sins*, and not for ours only but also *for* [the sins of] *the whole world*." 1 John 2:2 (emphasis added).

These are non-negotiable biblical facts. Isaiah wrote, "The chastisement for our peace was upon Him, and by His stripes we are healed." Isa. 53:5. "Chastisement" means "punishment." It was our "punishment" that Christ endured in Gethsemane and on that uplifted cross. In other words, what should have happened to us, *fell on Him*. What we deserve, *He endured.* He took our death sentence and *died in our place.*

Why did He do it? Because He loves us more than words can express. With a deeper longing than any earthly parent feels for a wayward child, our merciful Savior longs to forgive us, to release us from the condemnation of sin, and to transform our hearts and lives so we can someday live forever with Him in a better land.

All true Christians believe this, yet so many have failed to see the inescapable implication of the core biblical truth that "Christ *died* for our sins."

Think about it. If "the wages of sin" (Rom. 6:23) is conscious, unending, never-ceasing eternal torment, then the ONLY WAY Jesus could legitimately experience the full penalty for our sins would be for Him *to consciously suffer forever in our behalf.* "I'm so glad we don't have to sizzle forever," the righteous would then say throughout endless ages, "because God's Son is burning in hell right now for us!"

Do you see the point?

There's no way around it. To say that "the wages of sin" means burning forever, and then to deny that Jesus Christ is burning forever,

GOD'S INFINITE LOVE REVEALED

is to deny that Jesus Christ paid the full penalty for our sins. In that case, He really didn't. Instead, He would only have paid a mini three-day discounted price—between Friday and Sunday. But even then, diehard eternal torment advocates don't actually believe Jesus consciously suffered from Friday to Sunday anyway. At least I've never heard anyone say this. In fact, I don't think any Christian has ever believed that our Savior suffered in real flames at any time.

The only way to escape this unsolvable dilemma is to accept what Paul plainly wrote that "the wages of sin is *death*." Rom. 6:23 (emphasis added). This message was loudly proclaimed in Old Testament times whenever innocent lambs were sacrificed. Those animals *died*, and then portions of their bodies were consumed on Jewish altars. Period. That was it. On the cross, after six hours of unimaginable horror suffering God's just punishment for every sin we have ever committed, Jesus breathed His last breath. "It is finished!" (John 19:30), He shouted triumphantly. *Then He died.* Again, Paul wrote, "*Christ died* for our sins, according to the Scriptures." 1 Cor. 15:3.

Yes, Jesus Christ was *really dead*. But three days later, He rose *from the dead*.

SATAN'S FIRST LIE

The New Testament calls this "the Gospel," or Good News that must be proclaimed to all the world (see Luke 24:46, 47).

"We will never forget their sacrifice," Governor Schwarzenegger declared about those five heroic firefighters who perished in California. They didn't die for themselves, but for those they tried to protect and serve.

On an infinitely higher level, we must never forget Christ's sacrifice through which His unfathomable love for each of us shines forth. When we behold the magnitude of that solitary sacrifice, our hard hearts will soften, and we will be moved to repent of our sins and serve Him fully.

Why? Because He will torture us forever if we resist His pleadings? No, no, no! But because of His incredible love, tender mercy, and kindness so marvelously displayed. God seeks to draw us through love, more than to drive us through fear and terror. "And I, if I am lifted up from the Earth," predicted Jesus, "will *draw* all peoples to Myself." John 12:32 (emphasis added).

"Yes, I have loved you with an everlasting love," God tells us; "therefore *with lovingkindness I have drawn you*." Jeremiah 31:3 (emphasis added). His love is drawing us even now.

God's Infinite Love Revealed

God's true character—as revealed in the Bible—is a perfect blend of tender mercy and fair justice (see Exodus 34:5–8; Rev. 15:3). His true character is also called His glory (see Ex. 33:18). This is what Jesus Christ revealed throughout His life on Earth (see John 17:1, 6). In fact, God is so good and so merciful that He even allowed His own justice to fall without mercy upon His own Son so we might receive His mercy, be forgiven and live forever.

On the other hand, God is also so just that He wouldn't even let His own Son escape the death penalty. This is why Jesus died for us.

"Behold your God!" (Isa. 40:9) wrote Isaiah the prophet. In the bright light of our Savior's unfathomable suffering on a cruel cross for the sins of a lost world—which perfectly reveals God's mercy and justice—the everlasting verdict is in: "God is love." 1 John 4:8. Someday "The glory of the LORD [His character] shall be revealed, and all flesh shall see it together; for the mouth of the LORD has spoken." Isa. 40:5.

It is "the goodness of God," wrote Paul, that "leads you to repentance." Rom. 2:4. When the Holy Spirit penetrates our hard hearts with a revelation of God's goodness and glory, this will lead us to willingly drop to our knees, confess our wickedness, and trust Jesus as our Savior. Even more than this, as forgiven sinners, His grace will then enable us to obey His every command (which Adam and Eve failed to do) because we love and trust Him (see John 14:15; 1 John 5:3; Rev. 14:12).

It is this wonderful revelation of God's infinite love that Lucifer-turned-Satan so desperately seeks to hide from our eyes. If the Devil can somehow obscure our vision of God's goodness and glory, and of the truthfulness of His words, he can push us from Him and chain us to his side. If he can trick us into believing that God's commands are unfair, that the wages of sin *isn't* death, that we are all naturally immortal so we don't need to depend on our Maker to live forever, or that God is such a heartless monster who will torture us forever if we don't believe in Him—then will we never understand Him, or correctly reveal Him to others. Then the marvelous message that Jesus *really did die* for our sins and rise from the dead after lying lifeless inside a cold, clammy tomb—will continue to be obscured. Then we won't see His light.

All of these cunningly-crafted deceptions flow from Satan's first lie. Not only that, but they make God appear like a devil Himself.

Because of these devilish delusions about God's character, sin, the soul, immortality, and the true nature of Christ's sacrifice, Paul's prophecy is now being fulfilled worldwide:

> If our Gospel [Good News] is veiled, it is veiled to those who are perishing, whose minds *the god of this age has blinded,* who do not believe, *lest the light of the Gospel of the glory of Christ, who is the image of God, should shine on them.* 2 Cor. 4:3, 4 (emphasis added).

Yes, Satan really is deceiving "the whole world." Rev. 12:9. But he is a liar. We are *not* little immortal gods. Look closely: "He who has the Son has *life;* he who does not have the Son of God *does not have life."* 1 John 5:12. In other words, there is *no eternal life* for anyone without Jesus Christ. Never forget this.

It is my sincere hope that this brighter picture will be fulfilled in your heart:

> For it is the God who commanded light to shine out of darkness, *who has shone in our hearts to give the light of the knowledge of the glory of God in the face of Jesus Christ.* 2 Cor. 4:6 (emphasis added).

SATAN'S FIRST LIE

When we look into the face of Jesus, we will see that God isn't a cruel tyrant, but that He loves us more than words can express. The Devil will then be exposed as "a liar" and "the father" of falsehood (see John 8:44). But his day of reckoning is coming. Someday Satan and all who persistently choose to follow his crooked ways will be completely burned up (see Mal. 4:1, 3) in the lake of fire (see Rev. 21:8) and become ashes (see Ezek. 28:18), so that no trace is left of them. Then God's universe will be sparkling clean again, and His ransomed children will be happy forever.

> And God will wipe away every tear from their eyes; there shall be no more death, nor sorrow, nor crying. There shall be no more pain, for the former things have passed away. Then He who sat on the throne said, "Behold, I make all things new." And He said to me, "Write, for these words are *true and faithful.*" Rev. 21:4, 5 (emphasis added).

We will then live forever in Eden restored. But this time there will be only one special tree, "the tree of life" (see Rev. 21:1), *and no more Devil.*

God's Infinite Love Revealed

Now you know "the truth." John 8:32.
Let's thank God for it.
I hope to see you on the biblical Other Side.

THE END

SATAN'S FIRST LIE

To learn more about the "one thousand years" described in Revelation 20, read Steve Wohlberg's short booklet, *The Millennium: Shocking Facts about a Misunderstood Prophecy and Your Eternal Destiny.*

More Enlightening Books by Steve Wohlberg:

From Hollywood to Heaven
(Steve Wohlberg's Personal Testimony)

Secrets of Inner Peace

*Approaching Armageddon:
Discover Hope Beyond Earth's Final Battle*

The 666 Beast Identified

*The Bloody Woman and
the Seven-Headed Beast*

*End Time Delusions: The Rapture,
the Antichrist, Israel,
and the End of the World*

False Prophecies about Israel,

Babylon, and Armageddon

*God's Final Warning:
The Three Angels' Messages*

*The Truth about the Sabbath:
Discover Proof That the Seventh-day
(Saturday) Is Still God's Holy Day*

Decoding the Mark of the Beast

End Times Health War

Fabulous Health Made Simple

Juice Your Way to Fabulous Health

Sprout Power

Surviving Toxic Terrorism

*Demons in Disguise:
The Dangers of Talking to the Dead*

The Coming Judgments of God

The United States in Bible Prophecy

*Climate Change:
Is It the End of the World?*

Is God's Church Built on Peter?

Hidden Holocaust: Discover God's Love in the Abortion Nightmare

The Character of God Controversy

God Speaks Before the End of the World

*God's Last Message:
Christ Our Righteousness*

Will My Pet Go to Heaven?

Help for the Hopeless

White Horse Media Television Series
(Viewable on our YouTube Channel and
Available on DVD)

God: Fact or Fiction?

Weighing the Evidence

The Abortion Controversy:
Two Women Tell Their Stories
of Hope and Healing

Coming Out:
Former Gays Testify of God's Saving Love

Body Battles:
Protect Your Health. Avoid Dying Early.

Finding Hope in Depression and Despair

Preparation for the End-Times

Is Jesus Kosher for Jews?

Good News for Muslims

God, Satan, Money, and YOU

The Elijah Prophecy

Available From:
White Horse Media
P.O. Box 130
Priest River, Idaho 83856
1-800-782-4253
www.whitehorsemedia.com

Sign up for Steve Wohlberg's
free e-newsletter at:
www.whitehorsemedia.com

Follow him on Twitter:
@WhiteHorse7

Find him on Facebook:
www.facebook.com/stevewohlberg